GIANT BOOK OF JOKES

BY
JOSEPH ROSENBLOOM
ILLUSTRATIONS BY JOYCE BEHR

Sterling Publishing Company, Inc.
New York

2 4 6 8 10 9 7 5 3

Published in 1998 by Sterling Publishing Company, Inc.
387 Park Avenue South, New York, New York 10016

Printed and bound in the United States of America

Contents

Introduction

The important role that humor plays in helping the child to deal with language and logic has not been fully appreciated. It is well accepted that physical play helps the child to discover what his body can and cannot do. Child development specialists have not focused nearly the same amount of attention on the role of word play in the acquisition of language and logic skills.

Even a brief look at the repertoire of children's humor reveals how much of it revolves around word play. During the course of such play, the child quickly discovers how language is riddled with vagaries of all sorts. He soon discovers there is no absolute relationship between things and the names we give to things. The discovery of such an irregularity produces laughter. It is what makes a joke funny.

The following joke, for example, takes advantage of the fact that the word "order" has two different meanings. In one sense "order" means decorum, in another it means a request for food service.

Teacher: Order, children, order!
Sammy: I'll have a hamburger and a coke, please.

Another type of joke depends on the homonym. In the English language, unlike other languages, different words may be spelled differently but can sound alike. The following joke depends on the confusion between "heard" and "herd."

City Boy: Look at that bunch of cows.
Farmer: Not bunch, herd.
City Boy: Heard what?
Farmer: Of cows.
City Boy: Sure, I've heard of cows.
Farmer: No, I mean a cow herd.
City Boy: Why should I care? I have no secrets from them.

Genuine learning takes place during word play. Humor directs the attention of the hearer to hitherto unperceived aspects of language or logic and strengthens existing knowledge. While the joke may be fun— and it must be fun if it is to be a good joke—it is also an opportunity for a serious learning experience. The knowledge developed during the course of informal word play helps to reinforce similar skills acquired in the more formal contex of the classroom.

Since what is funny to one child may not be to another, the present collection includes as many different kinds of jokes and joke forms as possible. The jokes range from simple one-liners to elaborate story jokes. There are classic jokes every jokester should know as well as spanking new ones. It is hoped that this collection of well over 1,000 jokes will meet the needs of all readers, no matter what age or grade level, or taste in humor.

Joseph Rosenbloom

1
Quickies

Advice to worms: Sleep late!

Did you hear about the cannibal who liked to stop where they serve truck drivers?

Doorman: Your car is at the door, sir.
Car Owner: Yes, I hear it knocking.

Flip: Do you live in a small house?
Flop: Small! Ours is the only house in town with round-
shouldered mice.

Patient: Doctor, will you treat me?
Doctor: Absolutely not! You'll have to pay the same as everyone
else.

Silly: What did the police do when two hundred hares escaped
from the rabbit farm?
Sillier: They combed the area.

There is a new book out called *How To Be Happy Without Money* . . . It costs ten dollars.

Sign on a cleaning store specializing in gloves:
    WE CLEAN YOUR DIRTY KIDS!

One skeleton to the other:
    "If we had any guts, we'd get out of here."

Father to son:
    I don't care if the basement wall is cracking. Please stop telling everyone you come from a broken home.

    Did you hear about the snake charmer who married an undertaker? They now have towels marked "Hiss" and "Hearse."

Flip: If you were in a jungle by yourself and an elephant
      charged you, what would you do?
Flop: Pay him.

   "Hello, Operator, I'd like to speak to the king of the
jungle."
   "I'm very sorry, but the lion is busy."

Tip: Please tell me the story about the girl who bleached her
     hair.
Top: Absolutely not. I never tell off-color stories.

   Happiness is a warm puppy . . . doing it on someone
else's lap.

ADVERTISEMENT:
   For Sale: Large crystal vase by lady slightly cracked!

   My dog likes to eat garlic. Now his bark is *much* worse
than his bite.

   They laughed when they saw me sit down at the piano
with both hands tied behind my back. They didn't know I
played by ear.

   You'll be revered one day, Paul.

   I don't give a fig about you, Newton.

Famous last words of Eli Whitney:
   "Keep your cotton-pickin' hands off my gin."

Popular monster song:

"A pretty ghoul is like a malady . . ."

Mother monster to little son:

Please don't set in that chair! We're saving it for Rigor Mortis to set in.

Sign outside a restaurant:

DON'T STAND OUTSIDE AND BE MISERABLE—
COME INSIDE AND BE FED UP.

My cellar is so damp, when I lay a mousetrap, I catch fish.

Nip: The garbage man is here.
Tuck: Tell him we don't want any.

Sign in a restaurant window:

EAT NOW—PAY WAITER.

Teacher: Spell Tennessee, Johnny.
Johnny: One-a-see, two-a-see . . .

As the man said when he dented his new car, "Oh, well, that's the way the Mercedes-Benz."

Porky Pig: I never sausage heat.
Priscilla Pig: Yes, I'm almost bacon.

Old refrigerators never die, they just lose their cool.

I was teacher's pet.
She couldn't afford a dog.

Wise man says:
    The bigger the summer vacation, the harder the fall.

    Show me a dog in the middle of a muddy road, and I'll
show you a mutt in a rut.

    Hot weather never bothers me. I just throw the
thermometer out the window and watch the temperature drop.

Show me a pink polka-dot pony, and I'll show you a horse of a different color.

Show me a thirsty tailor, and I'll show you a dry cleaner.

Teacher: Joseph, name two pronouns.
Joseph: Who, me?
Teacher: Correct!

Clara: Do you realize it takes three sheep to make one sweater?
Sarah: I didn't even know they could knit.

My dog is a terrible bloodhound. I cut my hand once and he fainted.

Ernie: Does your dog have a license?
Bernie: No, she's not old enough to drive.

Wise man says:
    When in doubt, mumble.

Nit: Blood is thicker than water.
Wit: So is toothpaste.

    The study of language can be ridiculous sometimes.
I heard of someone who is beginning Finnish.

    He didn't know the meaning of the word "fear." (He was
too afraid to ask.)

    To waiter: Who made this Caesar salad—Brutus?

    Did you hear about the hippie who starved to death
rather than have a square meal?

    "Waiter, please get that fly out of my soup. I want to dine
alone."

    Why don't you go to a tailor and have a fit?

    There's a scale over there. Go weigh!

    Why don't you learn to play the guitar and stop picking
on me?

    Are you a man or a mouse? Squeak up!

Flap: Hello, old top! New car?
Jack: No, old car. New top!

Taxi Driver: Look outside and see if my blinker is on.
Passenger: Yes-no-yes-no-yes-no.

Sign in car wrecker's lot:

RUST IN PEACE.

Did you hear about the elephant who went to the beach to see something new in trunks?

Doctor: How did you get here so fast?
Patient: Flu.

Patient: What does the X-ray of my head show?
Doctor: Nothing.

"I told you not to swallow!" yelled the dentist. "That was my last pair of pliers."

Sign in a nursery:

ALL BABIES ARE SUBJECT TO CHANGE WITHOUT NOTICE.

No matter how you feel about warts, they have a way of growing on you.

Doctor: Did you take the patient's temperature?
Nurse: No, is it missing?

He's so weak, when he tries to whip cream, the cream wins.

NEW—FOR CHRISTMAS

A twelve-foot pole for people who wouldn't touch things with a ten-foot pole.

A new spinning top that is also a whistle. Now you can blow your top!

A new doctor doll. You wind it up and it operates on batteries.

Waiter: These are the best eggs we've had for years.
Customer: Well, bring me some you haven't had around for that
    long.

Show me a doctor with greasy fingers and I'll show you a medicine dropper.

City Boy: Is it easy to milk a cow?
Farm Boy: Any jerk can do it.

Dit: My grandfather was a Pole.
Dot: North or South?

Nita: I lived for a week on a can of sardines.
Rita: How did you keep from falling off?

If the world is getting smaller, how come they keep raising postal rates?

First Cannibal: Am I late for supper?
Second Cannibal: Yes, everyone's already eaten.

Customer: Waiter, bring me some turtle soup and make it snappy!

Customer: Do you have pickled herring?
Waiter: No, but we have stewed tomato.

Waiter (to customer): Don't complain about the coffee. You may be old and weak yourself some day.

Ike: What a day! The hail came down in buckets.
Mike: The hail you say?

"Will you pass the nuts, teacher?"
"No, I think I'll flunk them."

Tots Talk Back

Sam had just completed his first day at school. "What did you learn today?" asked his mother. "Not enough," said Sammy. "I have to go back tomorrow."

A ten-year-old boy was told to take care of his younger sister while his parents went into town on business. He decided to go fishing and took his little sister along.

"I'll never do that again," the boy complained to his mother that night. "I didn't catch a thing."

Mother said, "I'm sure she will be quiet next time, if you just explain to her that the fish run away when there's noise."

"It wasn't the noise," the boy said. "She ate the bait."

Little Girl: I'd like to buy a puppy, sir. How much do they cost?
Store Owner: Ten dollars apiece.
Little Girl: How much does a whole one cost?

Billy: I got a hundred in school today.
Mother: That's wonderful, Billy. What did you get a hundred in?
Billy: Two things. I got fifty in spelling and fifty in arithmetic.

First Kid: Why don't you take the bus home?
Second Kid: No, thanks, my mother would only make me bring
       it back.

Junior: Pop, I can tell you how to save money.
Father: That's fine. How?
Junior: Remember you promised me five dollars if I got passing
       grades?
Father: Yes.
Junior: Well, you don't have to pay me.

First Kid: Boy, was I in hot water last night!
Second Kid: How come?
First Kid: I took a bath.

Little Igor: What does your mother do for a headache?
Little Boris: She sends me out to play.

An angry mother took her eight-year-old son to the doctor's office and asked, "Is a boy of eight able to perform an appendix operation?"

"Of course not," the doctor replied.

The mother turned to the boy angrily, "I told you so, didn't I? Now put it back!"

"Sam's parents are sending him to camp for the summer."
"Does he need a vacation?"
"No, they do."

A small boy went to school for the first time. When he came home, he was asked what school was like.

"Nothing much happened," explained the little boy, "except that some lady didn't know how to spell cat. I told her."

Mother: Johnny, what is all the racket from the pantry?
Johnny: I'm busy fighting temptation.

"Dad, where were you born?"
"Chicago."
"Where was Mommy born?"
"Dallas."
"And where was I born?"
"Philadelphia."
"Amazing how we three got together, isn't it?"

Harold was home from college for the holidays. He said to his little sister, Suzie, "Would you like me to read you a narrative?"

"What is a narrative?" Suzie asked.

"A narrative is a tale," Harold told her.

That night when Suzie went to bed, Harold asked, "Should I extinguish the light, Suzie?"

Suzie asked, "What does extinguish mean?"

"Extinguish means to put out," Harold explained.

The next day they were at dinner when their dog made a nuisance of himself.

"Harold," Suzie said, "would you take the dog by the narrative and extinguish him?"

Teacher: Willie, please spell the word "pole."
Willie: P-O-L.
Teacher: But what is at the end of it?
Willie: Electric wires. But I can't spell that yet.

Mother: Did you go to the party?
Daughter: No. The invitation said from three to six, and I'm seven.

Two young children stood in front of a mummy case in the museum. On the bottom of the mummy case they noticed "1286 B.C."

"What does that number mean?" asked the first one.

The second one thought a moment and said, "That must be the license number of the car that hit him."

A Texas lad rushed home from kindergarten class and insisted his mother buy him a set of pencils, holsters and a gun belt.

"Whatever for, dear?" his mother asked. "You're not going to tell me you need them for school?"

"Yes, I do," he replied. "Teacher said that tomorrow she's going to teach us how to draw."

Suzie: What time is it?
Father: Three o'clock.
Suzie: Oh, no, not again!
Father: What's the matter?
Suzie: I've been asking people for the time all day, and everyone I ask tells me something different.

Mother: Harold, stop reaching across the table. Haven't you got
　　　 a tongue?
Harold: Yes, Mother, but my arm is longer.

Junior: When I grow up I want to have a million dollars, a big
　　　 house, and no bathtubs.
Mother: Why no bathtubs?
Junior: Because I want to be filthy rich.

Doctor: The best time to bathe is just before retiring.
Kid: You mean I don't have to take another bath until I'm almost
    sixty-five years old?

A small boy explaining to his father why his report card was so
bad:

"Naturally I may seem stupid to my teacher, but that's
only because she's a college graduate."

A prisoner escaped from jail and said to a little boy he
met, "Hooray! I'm free! I'm free!"
"So what?" replied the little boy, "I'm four!"

Little Al: Ouch! My new shoes hurt me.
Big Al: No wonder! You have them on the wrong feet.
Little Al: But I don't have any other feet!

Mother: Did you thank Mrs. Smith for the lovely party she gave?
Little Audrey: No, Mummy. The girl leaving before me thanked
    her, and Mrs. Smith said, "Don't mention it," so I didn't.

"Can you read and write?" the woman asked Tommy.
"I can write," Tommy replied, "but I can't read."
"Well, then, let me see how you write your name."
Tommy wrote something on a piece of paper and handed
it to the woman.
"What is this?" she asked as she tried to make out the
scribbling.
"I don't know," Tommy answered. "I told you I couldn't
read."

Junior wrote a letter from camp:
>Dear Mom,
>What's an epidemic?
>Signed, Junior

Suzie: Mom, can I go out and play?
Mom: With those holes in your socks?
Suzie: No, with the kids next door.

I don't like spinach and I'm glad I don't like it, because if I did like it I'd eat it—and I hate the stuff.

A man was putting up a knotty pine wall in the living room. His young son was curious, "What are those holes for?" he asked.

"They're knotholes," replied his father.

"If they're not holes," the boy asked puzzled, "then what are they?"

Father: Well, son, how are your marks?
Son: Under water.
Father: What do you mean?
Son: Below "C" level.

Salesman (in front of house): Little girl, is your mother at home?
Little Girl: Yes, sir.
Salesman (after knocking without luck): I thought you said your mother was at home?
Little Girl: Yes, she is, but I don't live here.

Little Boy (on phone): My mother isn't home.
Caller: How about your father?
Little Boy: Not home, either.
Caller: Who is home?
Little Boy: My sister.
Caller: Will you get your sister?
Little Boy: Okay . . . (delay) . . . I'm sorry, but you can't talk to her.
Caller: Why not?
Little Boy: I can't get her out of her crib.

A boy went to the drugstore to buy a can of talcum powder.
The clerk asked, "Do you want it scented?"
The boy answered, "No, thanks, I'll take it with me."

Father: Billy, please take the dog out and give him some air.
Billy: Okay, Dad. Where is the nearest gas station?

Horace: Does your dog have fleas?
Morris: Don't be silly. Dogs don't have fleas—they have
      puppies.

Librarian: Sh-hh-hh! The people next to you can't read.
Student: What a shame! I've been reading ever since I was six
      years old.

A little boy rushed by a policeman. Five minutes later he dashed by again. After he had raced by several times, the policeman stopped him. "What's the idea, Sonny?" asked the policeman. "Where are you going?"

The boy looked up and said, "I'm running away from home."

"If you are running away from home, how come you've gone around the block so many times?"

"It's the best I can do," the little boy said as he sped off again. "My mother won't let me cross the street."

Little Girl (answering phone): Hello!
Voice: Hello, is Boo there?
Little Girl: Boo who?
Voice: Don't cry, little girl. I guess I dialed the wrong number.

A small boy stood in front of the shoemaker's shop watching the man at work.

"What do you fix shoes with, Mister?" he asked.

"Hide," replied the shoemaker.

"What?" asked the boy.

"I said hide," replied the shoemaker impatiently.

"What for?" the boy asked.

"Hide, the cow's outside," the man said.

"I don't care if it is. I'm not afraid of a cow," the young boy replied.

Willie's father took him to the bird house in the zoo. They came to the stork cage. For a long time Willie looked at the stork, then turned at last to his father and sighed:

"Ah, Daddy, he never even recognized me."

A little boy and his sister put on their parents' clothing. They went next door and knocked. When the neighbor answered, they said, "Mr. and Mrs. Brown have come to call."

Taking it all in her stride, the neighbor lady said, "Please do come in, Mr. and Mrs. Brown. Will you join me in some refreshments?"

After serving them milk and cookies, the lady asked, "Care for any more?"

"Thank you, no," replied the little girl. "We must be going home now. Mr. Brown just wet his pants."

Sam's mother heard that old Mrs. Jones was ailing. "Sam," she said, "run across the street and ask how old Mrs. Jones is."

"Sure!" said Sam.

A few minutes later Sam came back and said, "Mrs. Jones told me it's none of your business how old she is."

A mother brought her child to school to register him. However, the child was only five and the age required was six.

"I think," the mother said to the principal, "that he can pass the six-year-old test."

"We'll see," replied the principal.

Then, to the child the principal said, "Son, just say a few words that come to your mind."

"Do you want logically connected sentences," asked the child, "or purely irrelevant words?"

Junior: Can you write in the dark, Dad?
Dad: I think so. What is it you want me to write?
Junior: Your name on this report card.

Little Suzie: Daddy, are the people down the block poor?
Father: I don't think so.
Little Suzie: Then why did they make such a big fuss when their
      baby swallowed a quarter?

Mother: Suzie, have you finished putting the salt into the salt
      shakers?
Little Suzie: Not yet. It's hard work pushing the salt through all
      those little holes.

Little Suzie was learning to brush her teeth. She came to her mother and asked, "Mommy, how much toothpaste should I put on my brush?"

"Oh, about the size of a bean," the mother replied.

A little while later Suzie returned with toothpaste spread from cheek to cheek.

Mother shook her head and said, "I told you the size of a bean."

Suzie looked at the brush and back to her mother and said, "Oh, I thought you meant a string bean."

Mother: Suzie, why are you crying?
Suzie: My dolly—Billie broke it.
Mother: How did he break it?
Suzie: I hit him on the head with it.

Father: Who was that calling?
Junior: No one special, just someone who said it was a long distance from Tokyo, and I said it sure was.

Junior: Why does it rain, Dad?
Father: To make the flowers grow, and the grass and the trees.
Junior: So why does it rain on the sidewalk?

Mother: Junior, you've been fighting again! You've lost your two front teeth.
Junior: Oh, no, I haven't, Mother. I have them in my pocket.

Eye Doctor: There now, with these glasses you'll be able to read everything.
Little Boy: You mean I don't have to go to school anymore?

"Were you nervous about asking your father for a raise in your allowance?"

"No. I was calm and collected."

Mother: What are you drawing, Junior?
Junior: A picture of heaven.
Mother: But you can't do that. No one knows what heaven looks like.
Junior: They will after I've finished.

The telephone rang and little Suzie answered. It was her girlfriend.

"Can you call back in around fifteen minutes?" said little Suzie. "I can't talk now, I'm in the middle of a tantrum."

A three-year-old had received a severe sunburn which reached the peeling stage. His mother heard him saying to himself as he was washing up for dinner, "Only three years old and wearing out already."

3
Zanies

Nit: Can you telephone from an airplane?
Wit: Sure, anyone can tell a phone from an airplane. The plane
     is the one without the dial tone.

Ernie: There's a man outside with a wooden leg named Smith.
Bernie: What's the name of his other leg?

Nit: I just had ten rides on the carousel.
Wit: You really do get around, don't you?

Lem: That star over there is Mars.
Clem: Then that other one must be Pa's.

"Hello."
"Hello."
"Is that you, Sam?"
"This is Sam speaking."
"Are you sure this is Sam?"
"Certainly this is Sam."
"Well, listen, Sam. This is Joe. Lend me fifty dollars."
"I'll tell Sam when he comes in."

A man's car motor went dead as he was driving along a country road. He stepped out of his car to see if he could fix it.

A big cow came along and stopped beside him. She took a look at the motor and said, "Your trouble is probably in the carburetor." Startled, the man jumped back and ran down the road until he met a farmer walking. He told the farmer what had happened.

The farmer asked, "Does the cow have a big brown-and-white spot over her left eye?"

"Yes, yes!" cried the motorist.

"Oh, don't pay attention to old Bossy. She doesn't know a thing about cars."

Ike: What are all those chickens doing out in front of your house?

Mike: They heard I was going to lay some bricks and they want to see how it's done.

Nit: I know a restaurant where we can eat dirt cheap.

Wit: Who wants to eat dirt?

Moe: Have you had your dinner yet?

Joe: Yes. I was so hungry at seven-fifty-nine that I eight o'clock.

City Boy: Look at that bunch of cows.
Farm Boy: Not bunch, herd.
City Boy: Heard what?
Farm Boy: Of cows.
City Boy: Sure, I've heard of cows.
Farm Boy: No, I mean a cow herd.
City Boy: I don't care. I have no secrets from them.

A big, mean lion was walking through the jungle. The first animal he met was a monkey. The lion pounced on the poor monkey and asked, "Who is the king of the jungle?" The frightened monkey replied, "You are, O mighty lion!" So the lion let him go.

The next animal the lion met was a zebra. He pounced on the zebra and roared, "Who is the king of the jungle?" The frightened zebra replied, "You are, O mighty lion!" So the lion let him go.

The lion walked on until he met an elephant and asked the same question. The elephant grabbed the lion, twirled him around, and threw him fifty feet.

The lion picked himself off the ground. "Just because you don't know the answer is no reason for you to get rough."

Dit: What is the best way to mount a horse?
Dot: How should I know? I'm no taxidermist.

Joe: My aunt collects fleas for a living.
Moe: What does your uncle do?
Joe: Scratch.

A hillbilly and his son were sitting in front of the fire smoking their pipes, crossing and uncrossing their legs. After a long silence, the father said, "Son, step outside and see if it's raining."

Without looking up, the son answered, "Aw, Pop, why don't we just call in the dog and see if he's wet?"

Ding: They laughed when Bell invented the steamboat.
Dong: That goes to show you how much you know. Fulton invented the steamboat.
Ding: No wonder they laughed.

Patient: My stomach's been aching ever since I ate those twelve oysters yesterday.
Doctor: Were they fresh?
Patient: I don't know.
Doctor: Well, how did they look when you opened the shells?
Patient: You're supposed to open the shells?

Farmer Smith: Do you like raisin bread?
Farmer Jones: Can't say. Never raised any.

Nit: Should you eat fried chicken with your fingers?
Wit: No, you should eat your fingers separately.

Moe: What are you reading?
Joe: I'm reading about electricity.
Moe: Current events?
Joe: No, light reading.

Farmer: This is a dogwood tree.
City Man: How can you tell?
Farmer: By its bark.

Sam: My puppy has a pedigree.
Pam: Do you have papers for it?
Sam: Of course, all over the house.

Ernie: I can't believe my eyes! There's a dog on Main Street
 handing out parking tickets.
Bernie: Is it a brown dog with pointy ears and a long tail?
Ernie: Yes, it is.
Bernie: Well, no wonder, that's the town police dog!

A man walked up to the delivery window at the post office, where a new clerk was sorting mail.

"Any mail for Mike Howe?" the man asked.

The clerk ignored him, and the man repeated the question in a louder voice. Without looking up, the clerk replied, "No, none for your cow, and none for your horse, either!"

Passenger: Is this my train?
Conductor: No, sir, it belongs to the railroad company.
Passenger: Don't be funny! Can I take this train to Boston?
Conductor: No, sir, it's much too heavy.

Sheriff to Cowboy: Quick—did you see which way the
    computer programmer went?
Cowboy: He went data way!

First Vampire: A panhandler came up to me yesterday and told
    me he hadn't had a bite in days.
Second Vampire: So what did you do?
First Vampire: What could I do? I bit him.

Customer: I'd like to buy some steak, but make it lean, please.
Butcher: Which way do you want it to lean, right or left?

    "What's one and one?"
    "Two."
    "What's four minus two?"
    "Two."
    "Who wrote *Tom Sawyer*?"
    "Twain."
    "Now say all the answers together."
    "Two, two, train."
    "Have a nice trip!"

Tutti: I can't sleep. What shall I do?
Frutti: Lie near the edge of the bed, and you'll drop right off.

    Have you ever stopped to wonder why goods sent by ship
are called cargo, but goods sent by the car are a shipment?

Mother: You're cleaning up the spilled coffee with cake?
Daughter: Of course, Mother. It's sponge cake.

Patient: Doctor, I need help.
Psychiatrist: What's the problem?
Patient: I think I'm a dog.
Psychiatrist: Please come into my office and lie down on the
    couch.
Patient: I can't. I'm not allowed on the furniture.

Bob: I know the capital of North Carolina.
Ray: Really?
Bob: No, Raleigh.

Waiter: Would you like a hero sandwich?
Customer: No, thanks, I'm the chicken type myself.

Tip: You can't drive that nail into the wall with a hairbrush.
Top: Really?
Tip: Of course. Use your head.

    A customer entered a music store and asked the sales clerk if he carried pianos.

    "Not if I can get out of it," the clerk replied. "I'm not strong enough."

Wise man says:
    Bird in hand makes it hard to blow nose.

Nit: Where shall we meet?
Wit: Under the clothesline.
Nit: Why under the clothesline?
Wit: That's where I hang out.

Boy: Where were you when the parade went by?
Girl: I was home waving my hair.
Boy: That's stupid. Next time use a flag.

Sue: I found a horseshoe.

Lou: Do you know that means good luck?

Sue: It may be good luck for me, but some poor horse is
running around in his stocking feet.

Lem: What are you doing?

Clem: I'm painting a picture of a cow eating grass.

Lem: Where is the grass?

Clem: The cow ate it.

Lem: Where is the cow?

Clem: The cow left. Why should it hang around after all the
grass is gone?

Caller (on phone): Hello? Is this the Weather Bureau?
Weather Bureau: Yes, it is.
Caller: How about a shower tonight?
Weather Bureau: It's all right with us. Take one if you need one.

Juliet (to Romeo): If you had gotten orchestra seats like I asked you, I wouldn't be up on this balcony.

Lem: I had a terrible nightmare last night.
Clem: What did you dream about?
Lem: I dreamt I was eating shredded wheat.
Clem: Why should that upset you?
Lem: When I woke up, half the mattress was gone.

Izzy: Did you hear the big noise this morning?
Dizzy: No. What was it, the crack of dawn?
Izzy: Nope, it was the break of day.

Dit: Did you know that the way my room is arranged, I can lie in bed and watch the sun rise?
Dot: That's nothing. I can sit in my living room and watch the kitchen sink.

Lady (in paint store): Do you have any wallpaper with flowers in it?
Clerk: Yes, we do.
Lady: Can I put in on myself?
Clerk: Of course, if you like, but it would look better on the wall.

Sue: I just came from a big fire sale.
Lou: What did you buy?
Sue: Four big fires.

A man waiting for a bus held his hands about four inches apart. He got on the bus, and when the driver asked for his fare, the man told him to take the money out of his coat pocket. The driver did as he said and drove on.

The man walked to the rear of the bus and sat down, still holding his hands in the same position. A woman passenger turned to him and asked, "Were you wounded in the war?"

"No, I wasn't," he replied.

"Then why are you holding your hands like that?"

"Because I'm on my way to a hardware store and I need a piece of pipe this long."

Fuzzie: Want to hear a couple of dillies?
Wuzzie: Sure!
Fuzzie: Dilly, dilly.

Mutt: Hello?
　　　—You don't say!
　　　—You don't say! (He hangs up.)
Jeff: Who was that?
Mutt: He didn't say.

Tutti: May I sit on your right hand?
Frutti: You can for a while, but I may need it later to eat with.

Lem: You play chess with your dog? He must be very smart.
Clem: Not really. I beat him most of the time.

Dog Owner: I'm worried, Doc. What should I do if my dog has
      ticks?
Veterinarian: Don't wind him.

Moe: That's a mighty strange-looking dog.
Joe: He's a genuine police dog.
Moe: He doesn't look like any police dog I've ever seen.
Joe: Of course not. He's in the secret service.

A woman telephoned an airline office in New York and asked, "How long does it take to fly to Boston?"

The clerk said, "Just a minute."

"Thank you," the woman said as she hung up.

Flip: Every night I dream I'm flying.
Flop: Why don't you sleep on your back?
Flip: What? And fly upside down?

The thunder god went for a ride on his favorite filly.
"I'm Thor!" he cried.
The horse answered, "You forgot the thaddle, thilly."

Lem: Where is the park?
Clem: There isn't any here.
Lem: Then how come the sign says, "Park here?"

Ding: Why are you taking your ruler to bed with you?
Dong: To see how long I sleep.

Mutt: My feet are frozen and they're sticking out of the covers.
Jeff: You fool! Why don't you pull them in?
Mutt: Oh, no! I'm not putting those cold things in bed with me.

Sam: I snored so loud that I used to wake myself up. But I finally
     cured myself.
Pam: How did you do that?
Sam: Now I sleep in the next room.

Tip: What's a football made of?
Top: Pig's hide.
Tip: Why should they hide?
Top: No. The pig's outside.
Tip: Well, bring him in. Any friend of yours is a friend of mine.

A world traveler was lecturing the club about his adventures.

"There are some spectacles," he said, "that one never forgets."

"I wish you could get me a pair," one member of the club said. "I'm always forgetting mine."

A lady went to the pet shop to buy a sweater for her dog. The clerk ask for the shape and size of the dog. However, the lady could not describe the dog accurately.

"Why don't you bring the dog in so I can fit him properly?" the clerk asked.

"Oh, I couldn't do that," the lady replied, "I want it to be a surprise."

A dog was so clever his owner sent him to college. Home for vacation, the dog admitted he had learned neither history nor science, but added proudly, "I did make a good start in foreign languages."

"Okay," replied the owner, "say something in a foreign language."

The dog said, "Meow!"

Ding: I lost my dog.
Dong: Why don't you put an ad in the paper?
Ding: What good would that do? He can't read.

Iggy: When I sneeze, I put my hand in front of my mouth.
Ziggy: Why do you do that?
Iggy: To catch my teeth.

Fuzzy: Last night I put my tooth under my pillow. This morning
      I found a dime there instead.
Wuzzy: When I put mine under my pillow, I got a dollar.
Fuzzy: Well, you have buck teeth.

Ike: Why are you sleeping under that old car?
Mike: So I can wake up oily in the morning.

Reporter (interviewing famous matador): Is it true that the bull
    becomes irritated when you wave your red cape at him?
Matador: Actually, the cows are the ones. The reason a bull gets
    mad at the red cape is that he doesn't like being
    mistaken for a cow.

Mutt: I wish I were in your shoes.
Jeff: Why would you want to be in my shoes?
Mutt: Mine have holes in them.

A formation of geese was flying south for the winter. One of the geese in the rear said to another: "How come we always have to follow that same leader?"

"He's the one with the map," the other replied.

"One man's Mede is another man's Persian."
"Are you Shah?"
"Sultanly."

Nit: What was the tow truck doing at the racetrack?
Wit: Trying to pull a fast one.

Newlywed Wife: I baked two kinds of biscuits today, dear.
    Would you like to take your pick?
Husband: No, thank you. I'll just use the hammer.

Nit: I just flew in from Europe.
Wit: I bet your arms are tired.

Lem: I just sat down on a pin.
Clem: Did it hurt?
Lem: No, it was a safety pin.

Horace: What are you doing?
Morris: I'm drawing my bath.
Horace: I paint a little myself.

Girl: I'd like a triple vanilla ice cream sundae with chocolate
        syrup, nuts, and lots of whipped cream.
Waiter: With a cherry on top?
Girl: Heavens, no! I'm on a diet.

Nita: Did you hear about the girl who went on a coconut diet?
Rita: Did she lose weight?
Nita: Not a pound, but you should see her climb trees.

Tutti: English food must be fattening.
Frutti: Whatever gave you that idea?
Tutti: I read in the paper about a woman in London who lost
        five hundred pounds.

Mr. Monster woke at midnight in a terrible temper.
"Where's my supper?" he yelled at his wife. "Where are my
chains? Where is my poison? Where is my . . .?"
        "Now wait a minute," Mrs. Monster replied. "Can't you
see I only have three hands?"

Two boys were boasting.

First Boy: You know the Panama Canal? Well, my father dug the hole for it.

Second Boy: You know the Dead Sea? Well, my father killed it.

Biff: London is the foggiest place in the world.

Boff: Oh, no, it isn't. I've been in a place much foggier than London.

Biff: Where was that?

Boff: I don't know, it was too foggy to tell.

Flip: What happened to your car? It's all banged up!

Flop: I was out driving and hit a cow.

Flip: A Jersey?

Flop: I don't know. I didn't get its license.

Igor: Why do you call your pet fawn "Ninety-Nine Cents?"

Boris: Because it's not old enough to be a buck.

Mutt: How much money do you have with you?

Jeff: Oh, between $48 and $50.

Mutt: Isn't that a lot of money to be carrying around?

Jeff: No, $2 isn't much.

Customer: Waiter! I just found this hair in my turtle soup.

Waiter: Well, well! So the turtle and the hair finally did get together.

Doctor: Ever had an accident?

Farmer: No.

Doctor: Never had an accident in your whole life?

Farmer: Well, last spring I was out in the field and the bull tossed me over the fence.

Doctor: Don't you call that an accident?

Farmer: No, the bull did it on purpose.

First Farmer: My scarecrow is so natural that it frightened every crow off the farm.

Second Farmer: That's nothing. The one on our farm scared the crows so much they brought back all the corn they stole last year.

Ike: This match won't light.
Mike: What's the matter with it?
Ike: I don't really know—it lit before.

A fisherman carrying a lobster bumped into a friend on the way home.

"Where are you going with that lobster under your arm?" asked his friend.

The fisherman answered, "I'm taking him home to dinner."

Just then the lobster spoke up: "I've already had my dinner. Can we go to a movie instead?"

A lady was invited to a costume party. She went to a store to rent a costume. The manager of the store showed her a beautiful princess costume with gown, lovely shoes, and a crown.

The lady asked, "How much?"

The manager said, "Twenty dollars."

The lady hadn't expected to spend that much, so she asked to see something cheaper.

Next the manager brought out a plain dress.

"How much?" the lady asked.

"Ten dollars," the manager replied.

This was still more than she expected to pay.

By this time the manager was becoming impatient. "I have the perfect thing for you," he said. "For one dollar, I'll give you a broomstick and a can of red paint."

"That sounds reasonable to me," said the lady, "but what do I do with it?"

"Stick the broomstick in your mouth," answered the manager, "pour the red paint all over your head, and go as a candy apple."

Beggar: I haven't had more than one meal a day all week, lady.
Fat Lady: Oh, how I wish I had your will power.

Dit: Peculiar, isn't it?
Dot: What is peculiar?
Dit: A person can walk a mile without moving more than two
    feet.

Flip: Are your blinds drawn?
Flop: No, they're real blinds.

It was the man's first trip by airplane. He was frightened and nervous. As the engines began to roar, he gripped the arms of his seat, closed his eyes, and counted to one hundred.

When he opened his eyes he looked out of the window. "See those tiny people down there," he said to the woman sitting next to him, "don't they look like ants?"

"They are ants," the woman said. "We haven't left the ground yet."

Ned: Did I ever tell you about the time I came face to face with a ferocious lion?
Fred: No, what happened?
Ned: There I stood alone, without a gun. The lion crept closer and closer and closer . . .
Fred: Then what did you do?
Ned: What could I do? I moved on to the next cage.

Moe: I've been seeing spots before my eyes lately.
Joe: Have you seen a doctor?
Moe: No, just spots.

Patient: Doctor, I haven't been able to sleep for a week. Every night I dream of a door with a sign on it. I push and I push—but I still can't open it.
Doctor: What does the sign say?
Patient: "Pull."

An accountant got out of bed one morning and complained that he had not slept a wink.

"Why didn't you count sheep?" his wife asked.

"I did, and that's what got me into trouble," the accountant replied. "I made a mistake during the first hour, and it took until this morning to correct it."

Flora: My husband has dreadful table manners. He always holds his little pinky out when he holds a cup of tea.

Dora: In society it is considered polite to hold out your little pinky when drinking tea.

Flora: With the teabag hanging from it?

A cowboy was leading a flock of sheep down Main Street when he was ordered to stop by the town policeman.

"What's wrong?" the cowboy asked. "I was just heading my ewes into a side street."

"That's the trouble," the policeman replied. "No ewe turns permitted on Main Street."

A cowboy was riding his horse when he saw a little dog running down the road.

"Hi!" said the dog.

"Hi!" replied the surprised cowboy. "I didn't know dogs could talk."

His horse turned his head and said, "You learn something new every day, don't you?"

A husband brought his wife to the doctor.
Husband: My wife thinks she's a chicken.
Doctor: That's terrible. How long has she been this way?
Husband: For three years.
Doctor: Why didn't you bring her to see me sooner?
Husband: We needed the eggs.

Tutti: Did you see me when I passed by?
Frutti: Yes, I did.
Tutti: You never saw me before in your life, did you?
Frutti: I don't think so.
Tutti: Then how did you know it was me?

Mrs. Jones: Is your house warm?
Mrs. Smith: It should be—the painters gave it three coats last
   week.

A mouse was dancing madly on top of a jar of jam. Another mouse came along and asked him why he was dancing.

"Can't you read?" replied the first mouse. "It says, 'Twist to Open.'"

A man bought a mousetrap. When he brought it home, he discovered that he had no cheese to bait it with. So he found a picture of some cheese, and put the picture in the trap.

The next morning he went to the trap to see if it had caught anything. The picture of the cheese was gone. In its place was a picture of a mouse.

Dit: A snake just snapped at me.
Dot: Don't be silly. Snakes don't snap.
Dit: This one did. It was a garter snake.

A man was sitting on his porch rocking back and forth. He seemed to be having a long discussion with himself. Every once in a while he broke into loud laughter. At other times, he shouted "Phooey" in disgust.

A policeman passing by stopped to watch the man and asked him what was going on. "I'm telling myself jokes," the man told him. "And if I say so myself, most of them are very funny."

"Then why do you keep saying 'phooey'?" the policeman asked.

"I only say that when I heard 'em before."

Biff: Can you tell me what time it is? I was invited to a birthday party and my watch isn't going.
Boff: Why? Wasn't your watch invited?

4
That's Entertainment

Mr. Magic: I can turn this handkerchief into a flower.
Little Boy: That's nothing. I can walk down the street and turn into an alley.

A magician finished eating a rabbit stew and rushed out of the restaurant saying to the waiter, "That rabbit stew made me sick."

The waiter, looking at him run, said, "Well, that must be the first time a rabbit ever made a magician disappear."

Interviewer: Tell me, Ali Baba, what is it like, flying on a magic carpet?
Ali Baba: Rugged.

Customer (at carnival): That knife-throwing act was terrible. I want my money back.
Carnival Owner: What was the matter with it?
Customer: Call that a knife-thrower? He got ten chances and he didn't even hit that girl once!

A magician performed his magic act on a luxury ship every evening. Also on board the ship was a parrot which belonged to one of the sailors. Every time the magician went into his act, the parrot screamed, "Phony! Phony!"

One day the ship sank. All that was left was the parrot sitting on one end of a log and the magician on the other end. The parrot turned to the magician and said, "Okay, wise guy, what did you do with the ship?"

The most popular sideshow in the circus was a horse that played jazz piano.

A farmer who saw the show was amazed. He asked the horse's trainer how the horse learned to play.

"No mystery," the trainer explained, "he took lessons for years."

Ike: Did you hear what happened at the flea circus?
Mike: No, what happened?
Ike: A dog came along and stole the show.

Newspaper headline:
    Local Man Takes First Prize in Dog Show.

    On their way to the seashore for a weekend engagement, a trainer and his talking dog were speeding along in a new sports car when a police car started closing in on them.
    "Better pull up to the side of the road," the dog told the trainer. "And remember—when he gets here, let me do the talking!"

    Did you hear about the French horn player whose toupee fell into his instrument? He spent the rest of the concert blowing his top.

Dit: Do you know what the elephant rock and roll star said into the microphone?
Dot: No, what?
Dit: Tusking—one two three; tusking—one two three.

Ernie: My uncle can play the piano by ear.
Bernie: That's nothing. My uncle can fiddle with his whiskers.

Teacher: Where is the English Channel?
Pupil: I don't know. Our TV set only picks up local stations.

A dog walked into a theatrical agent's office carrying a small case. The dog asked for an audition. "Okay, let's see your act," the agent said.

The dog opened the case and out flew a butterfly who sang "The Star-Spangled Banner" in a rich baritone voice.

The theatrical agent was astonished. He promptly signed the act.

Five minutes later the dog returned. "I have a confession to make," the dog began. "I was not truthful with you and my conscience is bothering me. The butterfly did not actually sing 'The Star-Spangled Banner.' You see, I'm a ventriloquist."

An actor came into the agent's office and said, "My act is really different. I can fly."

He then flew up to the ceiling, circled the room a few times, and came down in a perfect landing.

The agent was not impressed. "Okay," he said, "so you can imitate birds. But what else can you do?"

Dancer: Can you stretch the music out a little longer?
Orchestra Leader: Sorry, but this isn't a rubber band.

Ned: What did you get the little medal for?
Fred: For singing.
Ned: What did you get the big medal for?
Fred: For stopping.

Did you hear about the new dance called the Elevator? It has no steps.

Did you hear about the composer who took too many baths? He began to write soap operas.

Sam was playing the piano for his friend Paul.
"Well, how do you like it?" Sam asked.
"I wish you were on the radio," Paul replied.
"You mean I'm that good?"
"No," Paul said, "because then I could turn you off.

At the end of a bad piano concert, the pianist proudly remarked that he played everything by ear. A member of the audience remarked, "That explains it. I didn't think those sounds could be made by human hands."

Then there was the classical pianist who was not a good speller. When she went out to buy something she left a sign on the door which said, "Out Chopin. Be Bach in a minuet."

Sign in a music store window:

GUITARS FOR SALE, CHEAP.
NO STRINGS ATTACHED.

First Monster: Are the monsters in your town ugly?
Second Monster: Oh, yes. We held a beauty contest last year and nobody won.

Did you hear about the sword swallower who went on a diet? He was on pins and needles for six months.

Mutt: I was operated on last week and I really enjoyed it.
Jeff: How come?
Mutt: The doctor had me in stitches.

This was the actor's first big film role. In one scene he had to jump from a cliff a hundred feet high into shallow water. The actor took one look at the cliff and the water and refused to make the jump.

"What's the matter?" the director asked.

"I can't jump from that cliff," the actor insisted. "Do you realize there's only one foot of water at the bottom of the cliff?"

"Of course," the director explained. "You think we want you to drown?"

Announcer on TV horror theater:

"*The Invisible Man* will not be seen tonight."

Dit: Whatever happened to the lady you used to saw in half?
Mr. Magic: Oh, she's fine. She lives in San Francisco and New York.

Zip: Did you hear about the sword swallower who swallowed an umbrella?
Zap: No, why did he do that?
Zip: He wanted to put something away for a rainy day.

Arthur thought he was a great comedian. He was always looking for people who would listen to his jokes. The only trouble was that his jokes were awful.

One day Arthur was riding on a bus. A man got on and took a seat next to him.

"Want to hear some great jokes?" Arthur asked. The man said he didn't mind.

After fifteen minutes of the worst jokes he had ever heard in his life, the man asked Arthur if he made up the jokes all by himself.

"Absolutely," replied Arthur. "Out of my head."

"You must be," the man said as he got off the bus.

Lem: The last time I sang, my voice fell on a thousand ears.
Clem: Where were you singing, in a cornfield?

Actor: Have you seen me on television?
Acquaintance: Oh sure, I've seen you on and off.
Actor: How did you like me?
Acquaintance: Off.

Dick: I once sang for the King of Siam. At least that's what he told me he was.
Jane: Really?
Dick: Yes, he said, "If you're a singer, then I'm the King of Siam."

Sign on house: DRUMS FOR SALE.
Sign on house next door: HOORAY!

A trumpet player was blasting away in his apartment late one night. There was a knock on the door. He opened it and there stood his angry next-door neighbor.

"Do you know it is late and I have to get up early tomorrow?"

"No, I don't," the trumpet player said, "but if you can hum a few bars, I can fake the rest."

A goat was in the garbage dump looking for food. He discovered a can of film and promptly ate it. Another goat came along and asked if the film was any good.

"It was all right," the first goat replied. "But personally I liked the book better."

"How was that science fiction movie you saw?"

"You know, same old thing—boy meets girl—boy loses girl—boy builds new girl."

Ike and Mike went to the movies to see a film about horse racing. Ike said to Mike, "I'll bet you five dollars that number four will win the race." Mike agreed to the bet.

The horse won. But Ike said, "I can't take your money. I have to admit to something—I saw the movie yesterday."

"So did I," said Mike, "but I didn't think he could win twice in a row."

A father took his young son to the opera for the first time. The conductor waved his baton and the soprano began to sing. The boy watched everything with interest and finally spoke up.

"Why is the conductor hitting her with the stick?"

The father smiled and said, "He's not hitting her."

"Well," asked the boy, "why is she screaming?"

A baby rabbit kept pestering its mother. "Where did I come from, Mom? Huh? Huh? Where did I come from?"

The baby rabbit nagged until its mother finally said, "Stop bothering me, Junior. If you must know, you were pulled out of a magician's hat."

Small Boy: Mr. Magic, could you pull a rabbit out of your hat?

Mr. Magic: I'd love to, my boy, but I just washed my hare, and I can't do a thing with it.

Commercial:

Our product comes in two convenient sizes: 49¢ for the handy pint bottle and $2,000 for the large economy tank car.

Commercial:

Mother's Dill Pickles are untouched by human hands! You are probably wondering how she cuts them and stuffs them into the jars. Well, she has the longest and sharpest toenails you ever saw.

Radio Program:

Now for your morning exercises . . . Ready? . . . Up, down, up, down, up, down . . . Now the other eyelid . . .

"Step right up, ladies and gentlemen!" the medicine man at the carnival shouted. "I have in this bottle a miraculous fluid which I guarantee will help you live a long and healthy life. To look at me, you would never guess that I am over two hundred years old, would you? Know why I've lived this long? It's because I take a dose of this medicine every day."

A farmer thought he might give the medicine a try, but when he heard it cost five dollars a bottle, he hesitated. He got the medicine man's assistant aside and asked him if it were true that the medicine man was over two hundred years old.

"To tell you the truth, I don't know," said the assistant. "I've only been with him for the last one hundred and twenty years."

Commercial:

Have you heard about the new breakfast food for mothers? Instead of going "Snap, Crackle, Pop!" it goes "Snap, Crackle, Mom!"

The teacher asked his pupils to choose books on which to write a brief review. One lad chose the phone book. He wrote on his report: "This book hasn't got much of a plot, but boy, what a cast!"

"Pardon me, lady," the young man said in the darkness of the movie house. "Did I step on your toes a moment ago?"

"You certainly did," the woman on the aisle said.

"Good, then I'm in the right row," the young man said as he went back to his seat.

Agent (to writer): I've got some good news and some bad news.
Writer: First tell me the good news.
Agent: Paramount just loved your story, absolutely ate it up.
Writer: That's fantastic. And the bad news?
Agent: Paramount is my dog.

Proud Mother: Since he was a little boy, he always wanted to be
    a magician and saw people in half.
Friend: Is he your only child?
Proud Mother: No, he has several half brothers and sisters.

The chief of police in the small town was scolding his not-too-bright deputy.

"But how could you let the robber get away from you in broad daylight?"

"Chief, I couldn't help it. The robber ran into a movie theater."

"Why didn't you run after him?" the chief asked angrily.

"I would have, Chief, but I'd already seen the movie."

The movie was at a dramatic moment when a woman was disturbed by an old man looking for something on the floor.

"What have you lost?" the woman asked in an irritated voice.

"A caramel," the old man replied.

"A caramel!" she said. "Do you mean to say that you are disturbing me and everyone else for a caramel?"

"Yes," the old man explained and continued to look. "My teeth are in it."

5 Unfriendly Advice

A pesty child was making more and more of a nuisance of himself by playing ball in the aisle of an airplane. One man was particularly annoyed and finally lost his temper.

"Listen, kid," he said. "Why don't you go outside and play?"

Sign on newly seeded lawn:

DOGS BEWARE, VICIOUS MAN!

Patient: Doctor, I get the feeling that people don't give a hoot about anything I say.
Psychiatrist: So?

Mother (on phone): Doctor, Doctor! Junior has swallowed a bullet. What should I do?
Doctor: Don't point him at anybody.

Doctor: What is the problem?
Patient: I swallowed a roll of film.
Doctor: Don't worry, nothing serious will develop.

Customer: I have a complaint.
Waiter: A complaint? This is a restaurant, not a hospital.

Three boys walked into a candy store. The first one said, "I want a dime's worth of jelly beans."

It happened that the jelly beans were way up on the top shelf. The old storekeeper had to get a ladder and climb up, bring down the jar, count out ten cents worth of jelly beans, climb up and put the jar back. Then the storekeeper climbed down, put the ladder away and turned to the second boy.

"I want a dime's worth of jelly beans, too," said the boy.

So the old man got the ladder, climbed up and brought down the jar, counted out another dime's worth of jelly beans. However, before he put the jar back he had a thought. He said to the third boy, "Do you want a dime's worth of jelly beans, too?"

"No," the boy replied.

So the old man climbed up, returned the jar, climbed down, put the ladder away, and came back to the counter.

"Now," he said to the third boy, "what can I do for you?"

"I want a nickel's worth of jelly beans."

Teacher: Sam, what is the outside of a tree called?
Sam: I don't know.
Teacher: Bark, Sam, bark.
Sam: Bow, wow, wow!

"Mommy, all the kids say I look like a werewolf."
"Shut up and comb your face!"

A man was having trouble with a gopher in his yard. He went to the exterminator and asked him to get rid of the pest. The exterminator said, "I'd recommend the four-day process."

The homeowner had never heard of this process and asked how it worked.

"Simple," said the exterminator. "Every morning at seven you drop an apple and a cookie down the gopher hole. But at seven in the morning on the fourth day, you just drop in an apple. You wait five, ten, maybe fifteen minutes. All of a sudden the gopher will pop up, and when he asks, 'Where's the cookie?,' you clobber him."

Mrs. Jones: I'm sorry to bother you on such a terrible night, Doctor.

Doctor: That's all right. I had another patient down the road, so I thought I'd kill two birds with one stone.

Customer: Waiter, there is a fly in this ice cream.

Waiter: Serves him right. Let him freeze!

Slave master to Roman galley slaves who have been pulling on oars for hours:

I have some good news for you and some bad news. The good news is: You can have fifteen minutes rest. Now for the bad news: At the end of the rest period, the captain wants to go waterskiing.

First Rancher: What's the name of your place?
Second Rancher: The XWK Lazy R Double Diamond Circle Q
    Bar S.
First Rancher: How many head of cattle do you have?
Second Rancher: Only a few. Not many survive the branding.

Doctor: Ouch! OUCH!
Mother: Junior, please say "ah" so the nice doctor can take his
    finger out of your mouth.

A mother ran into the nursery when she heard her five-year-old son howling. His baby sister had been pulling his hair.

"Don't mind the baby," his mother said. "She doesn't know that it hurts you."

A few minutes later, the mother ran back to the nursery. This time it was the baby doing the screaming.

"What's the matter with the baby?" the mother asked.

"Nothing much," her five-year-old son replied, "but now she knows."

Insurance Salesman: You really should buy our accident
    insurance policy.
Customer: Why should I?
Insurance Salesman: Just last week I sold an accident insurance
    policy to a man. The next day he broke his neck and we
    paid out $50,000. Just think, you might be as lucky as he
    was!

Mother: How do you like your new teacher?
Little Girl: I don't like her very much.
Mother: Why not?
Little Girl: She told me to sit up front for the present—and then she didn't give me a present.

Father: Junior, I see by your report card that you are not doing well in history. How come?
Junior: I can't help it. The teacher always asks me about things that happened before I was born.

Teacher: Why are you crawling into class, Arthur?
Arthur: Because class has already started and you said, "Don't anyone dare walk into my class late!"

Doctor: How do you feel today?
Patient: Very much better, thank you. The only thing still bothering me is my breathing.
Doctor: We'll try to find something to stop that.

Horace: That is a beautiful stuffed lion you have there. Where did you get him?
Morris: In Africa, when I was on a hunting expedition with my uncle.
Horace: What is he stuffed with?
Morris: My uncle.

Tip: Did I ever tell you the story of my forebears?
Top: No, but I've heard the one about the three bears.

"Mom, what is a vampire?"
"Shut up, and drink your soup before it clots."

Sign in a pet shop window:

BOXER PUPPY FOR SALE.
HOUSEBROKEN, FAITHFUL, WILL EAT ANYTHING.
ESPECIALLY FOND OF CHILDREN.

First Invisible Man: Did you miss me when I was gone?
Second Invisible Man: Were you gone?

Truth Is Stranger Than...

Teacher: Let us take the example of the busy ant. He works all the time, night and day. Then what happens?

Pupil: He gets stepped on.

Tutti: He was once a lord who owned many castles. When he gave them up, he became very rude.

Frutti: Would you say he lost all his manors?

The dentist walked up to his patient, who let out a wild scream.

"What are you hollering for?" the dentist asked. "You're not even in the chair yet."

"I know, Doc," the patient answered, "but you're stepping on my corn."

A family that had spent its vacation on a farm the year before wished to return again. The only thing wrong with the farm was the noise the pigs made.

The family wrote to the farmer to ask if the pigs were still there. The farmer wrote back, "Don't worry. We haven't had pigs on the farm since you were here."

Flim: I paid a hundred dollars for that dog—part collie and part bull.
Flam: Which part is bull?
Flim: The part about the hundred dollars.

Harry: Didn't you say your dog's bark was worse than his bite?
Larry: Yes, I did.
Harry: Then for goodness sake, don't let him bark. He just bit me.

Lem: Don't be afraid. This dog will eat off your hand.
Clem: That's exactly what I'm afraid of.

Junior: Is it true we are made of dust, Mommy?
Mother: Yes, dear.
Junior: Is it true we turn back to dust when we die?
Mother: That's what the Bible says.
Junior: Well, Mommy, I just looked under my bed and someone's either coming or going.

Last year, 100,000 people died by gas: twenty-five percent were burned by it, fifteen percent inhaled it, and fifty-five percent stepped on it.

A horse walked into a soda fountain and ordered an ice cream sundae with chocolate ice cream and strawberry syrup, sprinkled with nuts.

The young man behind the counter brought the sundae to the horse, who finished it off with great pleasure.

Noticing how the young man stared at him as he ate, the horse said, "I suppose you think it strange that a horse should come into a soda fountain and order a sundae with chocolate ice cream and strawberry syrup, sprinkled with nuts?"

"Not at all," the young man replied. "I like it that way myself."

Irv: What are you up to?
Merv: I'm writing a letter to myself.
Irv: What does it say?
Merv: I don't know. I won't get it until tomorrow.

Nita: The trouble with you is you're always wishing for
      something you don't have.
Rita: Well, what else is there to wish for?

Lem: Did you hear about the turtle on the New Jersey Turnpike?
Clem: What was the turtle doing on the turnpike?
Lem: About one mile an hour.

Teacher (correcting a pupil):
      When I asked you what shape the world was in, I meant "round" or "flat"—not "rotten."

First Mouse: I finally got that scientist trained.
Second Mouse: How so?
First Mouse: Every time I go through that maze and ring the bell, he gives me something to eat.

Teacher: If you add 3,462 and 3,096, then divide the answer by 4, and then multiply by 6, what would you get?
Melvin: The wrong answer.

Teacher: Are you good in arithmetic?
Pupil: Yes and no.
Teacher: What does that mean?
Pupil: Yes, I'm no good in arithmetic.

A family of bears feeding in Yellowstone National Park looked up as a car crammed with eight tourists pulled up to the side of the road.

"It's cruel," Papa Bear said to his family, "to keep them caged up like that!"

A baby bear was born in the zoo yesterday and who do you think they sent to cover the story? A cub reporter.

Do Smokey the Bear posters help? Of course they do! Ever since they started putting Smokey the Bear posters in the New York City subways, there hasn't been a single forest fire in Manhattan.

Dit: I know a woman who is black and blue because she puts on cold cream, face cream, wrinkle cream, vanishing cream, hand cream, and skin cream every night.
Dot: Why would that make her black and blue?
Dit: All night long she keeps slipping out of bed.

Customer: And this, I suppose, is one of those hideous things you call modern art?
Art Dealer: No, it's a mirror.

The teacher asked the class to write a composition telling what they would do if they had a million dollars.

Every pupil except little Audrey began to write immediately. Little Audrey sat idle, twiddling her thumbs, looking out the window.

The teacher collected the papers, and little Audrey handed in a blank sheet.

"Why, Audrey," the teacher said, "everyone has written two pages or more, while you have done nothing. Why is that?"

"Well," replied little Audrey, "that's what I would do if I had a million dollars."

Boy on hands and knees looking for something.
Man: What are you looking for, young man?
Boy: I lost a dollar and I can't find it.
Man: Don't worry, you will. A dollar doesn't go very far these days.

Tourist: The flies are awfully thick around here. Don't you people ever shoo them?
Native: Nope, we just let them go barefoot.

His teenage daughter had been on the phone for half an hour. When she finally hung up, her father said, "Usually you are on the phone for at least two hours. How come this time the conversation was so short?"

"Wrong number," the daughter replied.

Customer: Waiter, this meat is bad.
Waiter: Who told you?
Customer: A little swallow.

Customer: Waiter, this coffee tastes like mud.
Waiter: Of course it does. It was freshly ground.

Teacher: How old were you on your last birthday?
Pupil: Seven.
Teacher: How old will you be on your next birthday?
Pupil: Nine.
Teacher: That's impossible.
Pupil: No, it isn't, teacher. I'm eight today.

Biff: I heard a new joke the other day. I wonder if I told it to
        you?
Boff: Is it funny?
Biff: Yes.
Boff: Then you didn't.

I know a lady who is so fond of arguing she won't eat anything that agrees with her.

Customer: Waiter, I can't seem to find any oysters in this oyster soup.

Waiter: Would you expect to find angels in angel food cake?

The U. S. Government reports that thirty million people are overweight. These, of course, are only round figures.

Teacher: Sammy, please give me an example of a double negative.

Sammy: I don't know none.

Teacher: Correct, thank you!

A little boy came home from his first day at school.
"I'm not going back tomorrow," he said.
"Why not, dear?" his mother asked.
"Well, I can't read and I can't write, and they won't let me talk—so what's the use?"

Baby Skunk: Can I have a chemistry set?
Mama Skunk: What! And smell up the house?

"I didn't send for a piano tuner," said the puzzled housewife.
"No," replied the piano tuner, "the people next door did."

A tourist stopped at a country gas station. While his car was being serviced, he noticed an old-timer basking in the sun with a piece of rope in his hand. The tourist walked up to the old-timer and asked, "What do you have there?"

"That's a weather gauge, sonny," the old-timer replied.

"How can you possibly tell the weather with a piece of rope?"

"It's simple," said the old-timer. "When it swings back and forth, it's windy, and when it gets wet, it's raining."

Igor: What do you have to know to teach a dog tricks?
Boris: More than the dog.

Ned: What kind of dog do you have there—a pointer?
Fred: No—a disappointer.

Flip: What do termites do when they want to relax?
Flop: They take a coffee table break.

Judge: The next man who raises his voice in the court will be thrown out.
Prisoner: Hip, hip, hooray!

Ike: Do you have holes in your underwear?
Mike: How insulting! Of course I don't have holes in my underwear.
Ike: Then how do you get your feet through?

Sam: My great-grandfather fought with Napoleon, my grandfather fought with the French, and my father fought with the Americans.

Pam: Your folks couldn't get along with anybody, could they?

Igor: Did you hear the story about the man who lives on onions alone?

Boris: No. But any man who lives on onions ought to live alone.

Two explorers were going through the jungle when a ferocious lion appeared in front of them.

"Keep calm," said the first explorer. "Remember what we read in that book on wild animals? If you stand absolutely still and look the lion straight in the eye, he will turn tail and run."

"Fine," said the second explorer. "You've read the book, and I've read the book, but has the lion read the book?"

Tip: Stop acting like a fool!

Top: I'm not acting.

A cannibal mother and her child heard the sound of an airplane and looked up. The child had never seen an airplane before and asked its mother what it was.

"It's something like a can of sardines," she explained. "You open it up and eat what is inside."

Ned: I just burned a hundred dollar bill.

Fred: You must be rich.

Ned: Not really. It was a bill from my dentist.

One day a lion came upon a bull wandering in the jungle. He pounced on the bull, killed him, and ate him. He felt so good afterwards that he began to roar. He roared so loud a hunter heard him, came into the jungle, and killed him.

So, when you are full of bull, keep your mouth shut.

Dit: Swimming is one of the best exercises for keeping the body slim and trim.
Dot: Did you ever see a whale?

Ecology is everyone's problem. A friend of mine went to the doctor for water on the knee. When the doctor made tests, it turned out the water was polluted.

Boy: Doc, my rabbit is sick. I can't understand it—I don't feed
    him anything but hair tonic.
Veterinarian: Hair tonic? That's the trouble. Don't you know
    you're not supposed to use that greasy kid's stuff on your
    hare.

Patient: You were right, Doctor, when you said you would have
    me on my feet and walking around in no time.
Doctor: I'm glad to hear you say that. When did you start
    walking?
Patient: Right after I sold my car to pay your bill.

Patient: My head is stuffed, my sinuses need draining, and my
    chest feels like lead. Can you help me?
Doctor: You need a plumber, not a doctor.

"My brother is so strong he tore up a pack of cards with one hand."

"That's nothing. My brother rushed out of the door this morning and tore up the street."

Have you heard about the new electric ruler? Turn it on and it rules the world.

Wise man says:
> You can fool some of the people all of the time, and all of the people some of the time, but the rest of the time they will make fools of themselves.

Learn from the mistakes of others, because you can't live long enough to make them all by yourself.

When everything's coming your way, you're probably in the wrong lane.

Nothing is all wrong. Even a broken clock is right twice a day.

Keep your words soft and sweet—you never know when you might have to eat them.

Show me a man who always stands on his own two feet and I'll show you a man who can't get his pants on.

Even Mason and Dixon had to draw the line somewhere.

Did you hear what the termite said when he walked into the saloon? He said, "Is the bar tender here?"

Teacher: Harold, if one and one make two, and two and two make four, how much do four and four make?
Harold: That isn't fair, teacher. You answer the easy ones yourself, and leave the hard ones for us.

Teacher: Why are you late, Joseph?
Joseph: Because of a sign down the road.
Teacher: What does a sign have to do with your being late?
Joseph: The sign said, "School Ahead, Go Slow!"

Then there was this guy who was so dumb he thought the Red Sea was parted with a sea-saw.

Biff: Only fools are certain. Wise men hesitate.
Boff: Are you sure of that?
Biff: I'm certain.

7 Crazies

Patient: Doctor, you must help me. I can't remember anything.
Doctor: How long has this been going on?
Patient: How long has what been going on?

Customer: Are you sure this ham was cured?
Waiter: Certainly, sir.
Customer: From its taste, I would say it's still sick.

Customer: Waiter, what kind of soup is this? I ordered pea soup, and this tastes like soap.
Waiter: My mistake, that's tomato soup. Pea soup tastes like gasoline.

Waiter: I have boiled tongue, fried liver, and pig's feet.
Customer: Waiter, I'm not interested in your medical problems. Just bring me a cheese sandwich and a glass of milk.

An excited woman telephoned her doctor, "Doctor, Doctor, my husband swallowed a mouse! What shall I do?"

"Wave a piece of cheese in front of his mouth until I get there," the doctor said.

Fifteen minutes later he arrived at the house to find the woman waving a sardine in front of her husband's mouth.

"I said a piece of cheese, not a sardine!" exclaimed the doctor.

"I know you did," the woman replied, "but I have to get the cat out first."

Farmer: On my farm we go to bed with the chickens.
City Man: In the city, we'd rather sleep in our own beds.

Larry and Harry went for a walk and they came to a large wall.

"How are we going to get over the wall?" Larry asked Harry.

Harry said, "It's easy. I'll shine my flashlight over the wall and you climb up on the beam."

"Oh, no, you don't," said Larry. "I'll get up halfway, and you'll turn the flashlight off."

Customer (at nut counter): Who's in charge of the nuts around here?
Clerk: One moment, please, and I'll take care of you.

A city man was driving in the backwoods of Kentucky when he took the wrong turn and got lost. He drove down a dirt road, hoping to find someone who might help him. He came to a fork in the road but couldn't decide which turn to take. Then he spotted a hillbilly rocking on a porch nearby.

"Hey, there!" he shouted. "Can you tell me where the road on the left leads to?"

"Don't rightly know," the hillbilly replied, continuing to rock.

"Well, can you tell me where the road on the right leads to?"

Again the hillbilly said he did not know.

The motorist became angry. "You're not very bright, are you?" he shouted.

"Maybe not," the hillbilly replied calmly, "but I'm not lost."

Doctor: What is the trouble?
Patient: I think I'm a dog.
Doctor: How long has this been going on?
Patient: Ever since I was a puppy.

Psychiatrist: What is your problem?
Patient: I prefer bow ties to long ties.
Psychiatrist: Is that all? Thousands of people prefer bow ties. In fact, so do I.
Patient: You do? What a relief! How do you like yours, boiled or fried?

Did you hear about the banker who could no longer ride a bike because he lost his balance?

An inmate at the insane asylum was sunning himself on the porch as a farmer passed by with a load of manure on his truck.

"Hey, Mr. Farmer," called the inmate, "what are you going to do with that load of manure?"

"Put it on my strawberries," the farmer called back.

"And they call me crazy!" the inmated chuckled. "I always use cream."

"I don't care who you are, fat man, get your reindeer off my roof!"

Teacher: How much is half of eight (8)?
Suzie: Up and down or across?
Teacher: What do you mean?
Suzie: Up and down it's 3, and across it's 0.

A deep-sea diver had just reached the bottom when an urgent message came from the surface: "Come up quick—the ship is sinking!"

Customer: Do you have frog's legs?
Waiter: Yes, sir.
Customer: Then hop into the kitchen and get me a sandwich.

Teacher: Can anyone name a deadly poison?
Pupil: Aviation!
Teacher: Aviation?
Pupil: Sure. One drop and you're dead.

A farmer advertised a donkey for sale cheap, and a customer questioned why the price was so low. The farmer said, "It's a good donkey, but it sits on eggs."

The customer considered this, decided he seldom had any eggs and bought the donkey.

He started for home riding the donkey and reached a bridge over a small creek, whereupon the donkey sat down. After much effort, he got the donkey up and headed him back toward the farmer.

"This donkey won't do," he said, and told the farmer what had happened.

The farmer wasn't surprised. "Oh, yes," he said. "I forgot to tell you he also sits on water."

Customer: Waiter, there is a button in my salad. I want to see the manager.

Waiter: Don't get so excited. It probably fell off while the salad was dressing.

Customer: What dishes do you have for me to eat?

Waiter (in a horrified voice): You eat dishes?

Woman: Doctor, please come quickly! My little boy has just swallowed a fountain pen.

Doctor: Of course, I'll be right there. What are you doing in the meantime?

Woman: Using a pencil.

Three men were sitting on a park bench. The man in the middle was reading a newspaper. The two men on either side were going through the motions as if they were actually fishing. They carefully baited their hooks, cast out the lines, and reeled them in when they had an imaginary bite.

A policeman stopped when he saw what was going on. Puzzled, he asked the man in the middle if he knew the two men on either side. The man folded his newspaper and admitted they were his friends.

"In that case," warned the policeman, "you'd better get them out of here!"

"Yes, Officer," the man replied, as he began to row furiously.

Sam: I'm having a lot of trouble with eczema, teacher.

Teacher: Heavens, where do you have it?

Sam: I don't have it, I just can't spell it.

A motorist, traveling in the country, found a bridge over a stream washed away. He noticed a hillbilly sitting nearby whittling away at a stick.

"How deep is this stream?" the motorist ask.

"Not too deep," the hillbilly replied.

"Think I can drive through it?" the motorist asked.

"Shucks, I reckon you can," the hillbilly replied.

The motorist, on hearing these words, got into his car and started across the stream. However, the car sank in the middle of the stream and he barely escaped with his life.

"What do you mean by telling me I could drive across?" the traveler said angrily. "That stream is at least ten feet deep."

The hillbilly scratched his head. "Funny," he said, "it only reaches up to the middle of the ducks."

A woman was taking a bath when she heard the front doorbell ring.

"Who is there?" she shouted.

"Blind man!" the voice replied.

Hearing this, the woman said she would be right there. Without bothering to put on clothes, she opened the door. There stood a surprised man, who said, "Where do you want me to put these Venetian blinds, lady?"

Two pigeons were flying over a used car lot. One said to the other, "Let's put a deposit on that Cadillac."

Junior: I'm so glad you named me Joe.
Mother: Why do you say that?
Junior: Because that's what all the kids in school call me.

Husband: This coffee tastes awful.
Wife: I can't understand why. It's fresh. I made it in my pajamas.
Husband: No wonder it tastes so funny.

Cannibal chief's wife to a friend: "Be sure to drop in Friday night. We're having the Joneses for dinner."

Joe: Do you still walk in your sleep?
Moe: Not any more. Now I take carfare with me when I go to bed.

Customer: Waiter, I'm hungry. Please bring me a mashed potato sandwich on rye.

Waiter: What are you saying? Only an idiot would order mashed potatoes on rye bread.

Customer: You're right. Make it on whole wheat toast.

Customer: Waiter, would you please put the rest of my steak into a doggie bag?

Waiter: Certainly. Anything else?

Customer: Better put some bread and butter in it, too, in case my dog wants to make a sandwich.

Customer: There is something wrong with these hot dogs.

Waiter: Sorry, sir, I can't help you. I'm a waiter, not a veterinarian.

Teacher: If I write *n-e-w* on the blackboard, what does that spell?

Sammy: New.

Teacher: Correct. Now if I put a "K" in front of it, what have we now?

Sammy: Canoe?

Sign at a garden center:

PLANT OUR SEEDS AND JUMP BACK!

Teacher: Lapland is thinly populated.

Pupil (raising his hand): Teacher, how many Lapps are there to the mile?

Policeman: What are you looking for, Mister? Did you lose
        something?
Man: Yes, I lost my watch.
Policeman: Where did you lose it?
Man: On Tenth Street.
Policeman: But this is Twelfth Street.
Man: I know. But when I dropped it, it was still running.

"Doc, Doc!" the man yelled. "I've got cucumbers
growing out of my ears!"

"My goodness!" exclaimed the doctor. "How did that
happen?"

"Sure beats me. I planted carrots."

Dick: I hear they gave out a lot of door prizes at the party last
        night.
Jane: They did.
Dick: Did you win anything?
Jane: Yes, four doors.

8 Disasters

Junior: Dad, can I have another glass of water before I go to sleep?

Dad: Another! This is your tenth!

Junior: I know, but my room is on fire.

Two lazy hillbillies were lying under a tree. One of them spotted a dangerous snake.

"Mind it there, Clem, there's a snake by your foot."

Clem slowly looked up and asked, "Which foot?"

A thief with a long record was brought before the judge.

Judge: Have you ever stolen?

Thief: Now and then.

Judge: Where have you stolen things?

Thief: Oh, here and there.

Judge: Lock him up, Officer.

Thief: Hey! When do I get out of jail?

Judge: Oh, sooner or later.

Did you hear the one about the tree surgeon who fell out of his patient?

The soldiers were in the thick of battle for weeks. The general gathered the soldiers together and announced: "Men! I have some good news and some bad news for you. First for the good news: Everyone will receive a change of socks!" On hearing this the men let out a wild cheer for their general.

"And now for the bad news: Kaminsky, you will change with Smith . . . Smith, you will change with Pirelli . . . Pirelli, you will change with Archer . . . Archer, you will change with Newton."

Aboard an airliner high over the Atlantic Ocean:

"Ladies and gentlemen! This is your captain. I have some good news and some bad news for you. First, for the good news: We have perfect visibility, clear weather, and we are making record time. Now for the bad news: We are lost!"

Zip: I almost drowned in my bed last night.
Zap: Are you kidding?
Zip: No, I'm not. The bedspread, the pillow slipped, and I fell right into the spring.

Ernie: I only got thirty-five in arithmetic and fifty in spelling, but I sure knocked them cold in geography.
Bernie: what did you get?
Ernie: Zero.

Horace: I know a man who was put in jail for stealing a pig.
Morris: How did they catch him?
Horace: The pig squealed.

Herman: Mother, can I change my name?
Mother: Why do you want to change your name?
Herman: Because Dad said that he's going to spank me as sure
        as my name is Herman.

Police Chief: The thief got away, eh? Did you guard all the
        exits?
Deputy: Yes, we did. But he tricked us. He went out through an
        entrance.

Most cannibal jokes aren't in good taste.

First Kid: My mother has the worst memory in the world.
Second Kid: She forgets everything?
First Kid: No, she remembers everything.

Did you hear about the writer who dropped eleven stories into a wastebasket and lived?

Teacher: How did you get that lump on your head?
Jimmy: I got hit by some beans.
Teacher: How could little beans give you such a large lump?
Jimmy: They were still in the can.

"Calling car 15! Calling car 15! Be on the alert. Someone just stole car 14."

Lem: They arrested the sword swallower and now he is in jail.
Clem: What did he do?
Lem: He hiccoughed and stabbed two people.

Newspaper story:
　　　The govenor's wife smashed a bottle of champagne
　　　against the bow of the ship as the crowd cheered and she
　　　slid into the sea.

Mother: Suzie, the salad tastes awful. Are you sure you washed
　　　the lettuce?
Suzie: Of course, Mom, you can still see some soap on it.

Ned: When I sat down to play the piano, they laughed.
Ted: Why?
Ned: No bench.

Snip: Look—there's a baby snake.
Snap: How do you know it's a baby?
Snip: I can tell by its rattle.

Dick: Did you hear about the accident at the army camp?
Jane: No, what happened?
Dick: A jeep ran over a popcorn box and killed two kernels.

Teacher: Jimmy, how do you spell "rain"?
Jimmy: R-A-N-E.
Teacher: That's the worst spell of rain we've had around here in
     a long time.

Nan: How did you make this cake?

Jan: Here's the recipe. I clipped it from a magazine.

Nan: Are you sure you read the right page? The other side tells how to make a rock garden.

Sign on used car lot:

SECOND-HAND CARS IN FIRST-CRASH CONDITION.

At the county fair, a pilot offered to fly anyone in his old, open-cockpit plane for five dollars. One farmer and his wife who had never been up in a plane kept hanging around, but couldn't decide whether to go or not to go.

"Come on," said the pilot. "I'll take you up for nothing if you're a good passenger and don't do any backseat driving."

The pilot took up the farmer and his wife and he did some pretty fancy flying. When he landed ten minutes later he said to the farmer, "You did very well for your first flight. I didn't hear a word from you."

"That's right," said the farmer. "It was pretty hard. I almost said something back there when my wife fell out."

Sue: I hear you cracked up your car. How did it happen?

Lou: See that ditch over there?

Sue: Yes.

Lou: Well, I didn't.

Did you hear about the man who sat in front of the electric fan with a BB gun because he wanted to shoot the breeze?

May: Did you hear about the guy who stole the calendar?
Ray: No, what happened?
May: He got twelve months.

A cargo ship loaded with twenty-five tons of yo-yos sailed across the Pacific. The ship ran into a fierce storm and sprang a leak. It sank and rose again forty times until it finally came to rest on the ocean bottom.

Ned: Did you hear about the thief who was caught in the rubber factory?
Fred: No, what happened?
Ned: The judge sent him up for a stretch.

Victim (after burglary): They stole everything from my house but the soap and towels.
Policeman: Why, the dirty crooks!

Little Georgie: Joe and I were playing at the well. Joe got into the bucket and the rope broke.
Joe's Mother: Good heavens! Did he drown?
Little Georgie: Don't get so excited. It was only a drop in the bucket.

Ding: Did you hear about the kidnapping down the street?
Dong: How awful! What happened?
Ding: Nothing much. After a while his mother woke him up.

Horace: I fell and hit my head against the piano.
Morris: Did you hurt yourself?
Horace: No. Luckily, I hit the soft pedal.

Tip: Why are you putting iodine on your paycheck?
Top: Because I just got a cut in my salary.

Dit: Clocks can be dangerous.
Dot: You must be joking!
Dit: No, I'm not. My clock just struck two.

Ike: I got fired from my job as a bank guard today.

Mike: What happened?

Ike: A thief came into the bank. I drew my gun and told him if he took one more step, I'd let him have it.

Mike: What did he do then?

Ike: He took one more step, so I let him have it. Who wanted that stupid old gun, anyway?

Judge: What do you mean by bringing a ladder into this room?

Criminal: I want to take my case to a higher court.

Lem: A woman fell overboard from a ship. A shark came up, looked her over, and swam away.

Clem: Why did the shark do that?

Lem: Because it was a man-eating shark.

Lem: Did you hear about the woman who got hurt while taking
    a milk bath?
Clem: How can anyone get hurt taking a milk bath?
Lem: The cow fell on her.

Horace: Jumping off the Golden Gate Bridge is not dangerous.
Morris: How can you say that?
Horace: It's a fact. Jumping off is not dangerous—it's the sudden
    stop at the end that is.

Flip: Did you hear about the man who was trampled to death
    by a herd of sheep?
Flop: No, what happened?
Flip: He sort of dyed-in-the-wool.

    "Mom, Arnold broke a window."
    "How did he do it?"
    "I threw a rock at him—and he ducked."

    Two men were resting after having donated blood at a
Red Cross station. One was a visitor to New York, the other an
Apache Indian. After staring at the Indian for a few minutes, the
tourist asked, "Are you really a full-blooded Indian?"
    "I was, but not now," replied the Apache. "I'm one pint
short."

    Laugh and the world laughs with you; cry and your
mother takes your temperature.

Father: Didn't you promise to be a good boy?

Son: Yes, Father.

Father: And didn't I promise to punish you if you weren't?

Son: Yes, Father. But since I've broken my promise, you don't
    have to keep yours.

Teacher: Tom, if you had one dollar and you asked your father
    for another dollar, how many dollars would you have?

Tom: One dollar.

Teacher: You don't know your arithmetic.

Tom: You don't know my father.

Ernie: Is it true you said you could jump off a cliff and not get
    hurt?

Bernie: No, that was just a bluff.

Aviator: First one wing came off and then the other.

Listener: What did you do?

Aviator: I grabbed a drumstick and had a second helping.

Squire: Is there anything I can do for you, Sire?

King Arthur: Yes! Make haste and fetch a can opener hither. I
    have a flea in my knight clothes.

Mother: Suzie, the cookies taste awful! Are you sure you put in
    a dash of salt?

Suzie: A dash of salt? Sorry, Mom, I thought you said a dish of
    salt.

Reassuring voice heard over the intercom of a jet plane:

"Ladies and gentlemen, please sit back and relax. This plane is entirely automatic. Automatic pilot, automatic food services, automatic landing devices. Nothing can go wrong . . . Nothing can go wrong . . . Nothing can go wrong . . . "

"I have some good news and some bad news for you, Daddy! First for the good news: You can take your hand off the leak in the pipe."

"That's a relief, son. Did the plumber get here?"

"Now for the bad news. We need the water because the house is on fire!"

9 Love and Kisses (Ugh!)

Two Martians landed on a corner traffic light.

"I saw her first," one said.

"So what?" the other Martian replied. "I'm the one she winked at."

Dick: What does *t-e-r-r-i-f-y* spell?
Jane: Terrify.
Dick: What does *t-i-s-s-u-e* spell?
Jane: Tissue.
Dick: Now both together, what do they spell?
Jane: Terrify tissue.
Dick: Why no—go ahead!

Did you hear about the two boas who got married? They had a crush on each other.

Mr. Wood and Mr. Stone were sitting on a park bench when suddenly a beautiful girl came around the corner. Stone turned to Wood, Wood turned to Stone, and the girl turned into a store.

He: If you won't marry me, I'll hang myself with a rope in front of   your house.
She: Please don't. You know my father doesn't like to have you hanging around.

Igor: You remind me of a pie.
Boris: You mean I'm sweet?
Igor: No, you have some crust.

Husband: My hair is getting thinner.
Wife: So what? Who wants fat hair?

A mother mummy was dressing her daughter for her first dance. The daughter was so excited she asked her mother, "Mummy, did they have dances when you were alive?"

Doctor: What seems to be the trouble?
Pretty Girl: I have a pain in my right side.
Doctor (after examining girl): You have acute appendicitis.
Pretty Girl: Don't get fresh, Doctor! Just tell me what's wrong.

Wise man says:
   A ring on the hand is worth two on the phone.

Did you hear about the couple who met in a revolving door? They're still going around together.

First Monster: That girl over there rolled her eyes at me. What should I do?

Second Monster: If you are a real gentleman, you will pick them up and roll them back to her.

He: I can't leave you.

She (blushing): Do you like me so much?

He: No. You're standing on my foot.

John (handing a chocolate): Here, honey, sweets to the sweet.

Mary: Oh, thank you! Won't you have some of these nuts?

Did you hear about the girl who went to the beach and baked herself under the hot sun for six hours? She wanted to be the toast of the town.

Father: The man who marries my daughter gets a prize.
Suitor: Can I see the prize first?

He: I'm going to marry a girl who can take a good joke.
She: That's the only kind you'll get.

Tracy: What is your new boyfriend like?
Stacy: He is mean, low, nasty, dirty and those are just his
      good points.

The young man was on his first date with the new girl. Things were going along well. As they rode along in his car, she turned to him and shyly asked, "Would you like to see where I was operated on?"
    The young man gulped and said, "Why, sure."
    "Okay," said the girl. "We're passing the hospital now."

He: Darling, will you marry me?
She: No, but I will always admire your good taste.

He: If you won't marry me, I'll blow my brains out.
She: Really? That would be a great joke on Dad. He says you
    don't have any.

He: Do you like my company?
She: I don't know. What company are you with?

First Monster: My girlfriend has pedestrian eyes.
Second Monster: What are pedestrian eyes?
First Monster: They look both ways before they cross.

"Everyone in the bus," the bus driver shouted so he could close the bus door and pull away from the curb.

"No," a female voice called "I'm not inside yet. Wait until I get my clothes on!"

Everyone in the bus turned to catch a glimpse of the woman. She finally managed to get on the bus—with a large basket of laundry.

She: Now that we are engaged, I hope you'll give me a ring.
He: Of course. What's your number?

The lady named her cat "Trouble." One night it sneaked out of the house. The lady was worried, and although it was past midnight, she went looking for her pet dressed in a nightgown.

She ran into a local policeman who asked what she was doing out at this late hour and dressed in a nightgown.

"I'm looking for Trouble," she said.

He: Here is the diamond engagement ring I got for you.
She: It's nice, but the diamond has a flaw in it.
He: You oughtn't to notice that. Aren't you in love, and isn't love blind?

Wise man says:
'Tis better to have loved a short girl than never to have loved a tall.

Mrs. Jones: I'm worried about my daughter. She's being chased
      by that wild new doctor.
Mrs. Smith: Have you tried giving her an apple a day?

She: Do you love me?
He: Madly! I would die for you.
She: You're always saying that, but you never do it.

10
Put-Downs

Clothing Salesman: That suit fits you like a glove.
Customer: Can you show me one that fits like a suit?

Ned: I feel like a million dollars.
Fred: You look like a million dollars—in counterfeit money.

Bill: I didn't come here to be insulted!
Phil: Where do you usually go to be insulted?

Nit: Please call me a taxi.
Wit: Okay, you're a taxi. But to tell the truth, you look more like
    a truck to me.

First Hunter: Be careful with that gun. You just missed shooting
    me.
Second Hunter: Did I? I'm very sorry.

First Woman: He kept my photograph over his heart and it stopped the bullet that bank robber fired at him.
Second Woman: I'm not surprised. Your face would stop anything.

I never forget a face, but in your case I'll make an exception.

Igor: I trace my ancestors all the way back to royalty.
Boris: King Kong?

Patient: Thank you, Doctor. Now I feel like my old self again.
Doctor: In that case you'll need more treatment.

Tip: I suppose you think I'm a perfect idiot?
Top: No, no one is perfect.

Ike: What time is it?
Mike: Sorry, but my watch is on the bum.
Ike: Yes, I can see that.

Igor: Commissar! Commissar! The troops are revolting.
Commissar: Well, you're pretty revolting yourself.

Horace: I can't get to sleep some nights. I've tried all sorts of remedies, but nothing seems to work.
Morris: Have you tried talking to yourself?

Mona: Whenever I'm down in the dumps I buy new clothes.
Lisa: So that's where you get them!

Iggy: Where do all the bugs go in the winter?
Ziggy: Search me.
Iggy: No, thanks. I just wanted to know.

Mrs. Smith: Have you told your little boy not to go around
        imitating me?
Mrs. Jones: Yes, I have. I told him not to act like an idiot.

Andy: Did the music teacher really say your voice was out of
        this world?
Sandy: Not exactly. She said it was unearthly.

    "Harry learned to play the piano in no time."
    "Yes, I heard him playing it that way the other day."

Flip: What do you mean—calling me deaf and dumb?
Flop: I never said you were deaf.

Tip: Isn't that a rare work of art?
Top: You are right, it's not well done.

Dit: Is that perfume I smell?
Dot: It is—and you do!

Iggy: When tourists visit my town, they come to see me.
Ziggy: Yes, you sure are a sight!

Nit: I wonder how long a person can live without a brain?
Wit: How old are you?

Dick: Don't you think I sing with feeling?
Jane: No. If you had any feeling, you wouldn't sing.

Mona: Whenever you sing, it reminds me of a pirate.
Lisa: How is that?
Mona: Murder on the high C's.

When your grandfather was born, they passed out cigars. When your father was born, they passed out cigarettes. When you were born—they just passed out.

Dit: Did your mother ever lift weights?
Dot: Why do you think that?
Dit: How else could she have raised a big dumbbell like you?

Fuzzy: What time is it?
Wuzzy: I have no idea.
Fuzzy: Yes, I know that, but what time is it?

Musician: Why do you play the same piece of music over and
 over?
Student: It haunts me.
Musician: It *should* haunt you, you've murdered it long enough.

Izzy: She's a real bargain.
Ozzie: How is that?
Izzy: Fifty percent off.

 She was going to have her face lifted, but she couldn't
find the jack.

Nita: I have a hunch.
Rita: And here I thought you were just round-shouldered!

Mutt: I understand that fish is brain food.
Jeff: Yes, I eat it all the time.
Mutt: Oh, well! There goes another scientific theory.

Proud Father: My baby is the image of me.
Bystander: What do you care, so long as it's healthy?

 He is so stupid he has to stand on his head to turn things
over in his mind.

Ned: Our dog is just like one of the family.
Fred: Which one?

Wise man says:
　　Better to keep your mouth closed and make people
wonder if you are stupid than to open it and remove all doubt.

Tutti: I don't know which to go to—a palmist or a mind reader.
　　　Which would you suggest?
Frutti: Better go to a palmist—at least you know you've got a
　　　palm.

She: You remind me of the ocean.
He: You mean wild, restless, romantic?
She: No, you make me feel sick.

Horace: Last night I dreamed I saw something in front of your
        house that made me very happy.
Morris: What was it?
Horace: A moving van.

He: I have music in my feet!
She: Yes, two flats.

Mutt: You look like a million.
Jeff: You never saw a million.
Mutt: Right! You look like nothing I ever saw.

Junior: I'm not going back to school anymore.
Mother: Why not?
Junior: On Monday the teacher said that four and four make
        eight. On Tuesday she said six and two make eight. Today
        she said that five and three make eight. I'm not going
        back until she makes up her mind.

Kitty: How do you like my new dress? I got it for a ridiculous
       price.
Cathy: You mean you got it for an absurd figure.

Tip: What's the idea of telling everyone I'm a jerk?
Top: Sorry, I didn't know it was a secret.

Horace: You remind me of London.
Morris: Because of my English accent?
Horace: No, because you're always in a fog.

Pupil: I don't think I deserve a zero on this test.
Teacher: I agree, but it's the lowest mark I can give you.

Gunman: Get ready to die. I'm going to shoot you.
Man: Why?
Gunman: I've always said I'd shoot anyone who looked like
     me.
Man: Do I look like you?
Gunman: Yes.
Man: Go ahead and shoot!

Fred: When I die I'm going to leave my brain to science.
Ned: That's nice. Every little bit helps.

Try These on a Friend—
If You Dare

Ding: Do you know the difference between a piece of candy
    and an old glove?
Dong: No.
Ding: Good. Then eat this old glove.

Biff: There is one good thing about the smog.
Boff: What's that?
Biff: At least you can see what you're breathing.

Dit: I haven't slept for days.
Dot: Aren't you tired?
Dit: Not in the least. I sleep nights.

Iggy: Want to see something swell?
Ziggy: Sure.
Iggy: Watch me blow up this balloon.

Lem: Did you ever hear the memory joke?
Clem: No.
Lem: Sorry, I forgot it.

Long: Is your refrigerator running?
Short: Yes.
Long: Better catch it!

Boris: I can lift an elephant with one hand.
Igor: I don't believe you.
Boris: Get me an elephant with one hand, and I'll show you.

Tip (sitting next to an empty seat): Will you join me?
Top: Why, are you coming apart?

First Kid: Something happened to me yesterday that will never
        happen to me again, even if I live to be a hundred.
Second Kid: What's that?
First Kid: I was twelve years old.

Lem: If a had a thousand men and you had a thousand men,
        and we had a war, who would win?
Clem: I give up, who?
Lem: I would win. You just gave up!

Horace: Do you believe in the hereafter?
Morris: Yes, I do.
Horace: Then, hereafter don't bother me.

Jekyll: Why did the rooster cross the road?
Hyde: I don't know.
Jekyll: To get a Chinese newspaper. Do you get it?
Hyde: No.
Jekyll: Neither do I. I get the *Evening News* myself.

Fuzzy: There is a new soft drink around called "Up Doc."
Wuzzy: What's "Up Doc?"
Fuzzy: Nothing much. What's up with you?

"I can stay under water for ten minutes!" (Your friend probably will say this is impossible. Then take a glass of water and hold it over your head.)

Jekyll: If you were in line at a ticket window, and the man in front of you was going to Chicago and the lady behind you was going to Atlanta, where would you be going?
Hyde: I don't know.
Jekyll: If you don't know where you are going, why are you in line?

Biff: Have you heard? Have you heard? It's all over the building.
Boff: What's all over the building?
Biff: The roof.

Jekyll: Did you hear about the boy and girl vampires who couldn't get married?
Hyde: No, what happened?
Jekyll: They loved in vein.

Harry: What are you going to give me for my birthday?
Larry: Close your eyes and tell me what you see.
Harry: I see nothing.
Larry: Well, that's what you're going to get for your birthday.

Flip: Why did the turkey cross the road?
Flop: I don't know, why?
Flip: To prove he wasn't chicken.

Iggy: Did you hear about the owl who went "tweet, tweet"
    instead of "who, who?"
Ziggy: No. Why did he go "tweet, tweet?"
Iggy: Because he didn't give a hoot.

Joe: If you were walking in a field and you didn't have a gun
    and you saw a bear heading for you, would you keep on
    walking—or would you run back into town?
Moe: I'd run back into town.
Joe: With a bear behind?

"If frozen water is iced water, what is frozen ink?"
"Iced ink."
"You do?!?"

"I bet I can jump across the street." (Your friend says you
can't. Walk across the street and jump.)

"Have you heard the story of the dirty shirt?"
"No."
"That's one on you."

"Did you hear about my friend Kerch?"
"Kerch who?"
"Gesundheit!"

"There were eight morons: do, re, fa, so, la, ti, do."
"Hey, what happened to 'mi'?"
"Sorry, I forgot about you."

First College Student: I'm studying ancient history.
Second College Student: So am I. Let's get together someday
    and talk over old times.

"I can speak any language in the world except Greek."
"Okay, let me hear you speak Chinese."
"That's Greek to me."
"Let me hear you speak Russian."
"That's Greek to me," etc., etc.

Horace: I can prove that you are not here.
Morris: I don't believe you.
Horace: I'll show you. Now, tell me, are you in New York?
Morris: No.
Horace: Are you in Chicago?
Morris: No.
Horace: Are you in Los Angeles?
Morris: No.
Horace: If you aren't in those places, you must be someplace
      else, right? And if you're someplace else, then you aren't
      here.

Little Al: I bet I can make you say "black."
Big Al: Okay, try it.
Little Al: What are the colors of the flag?
Big Al: Red, white and blue.
Little Al: I told you I could make you say black.
Big Al: I didn't say black.

    "Is Frank Walls there?"
    "No."
    "Is Pete Walls there?"
    "No."
    "Are there any Walls there?"
    "No."
    "Then what holds the roof up?"

Lem: You remind me of a shirt button.
Clem: How is that?
Lem: Always popping off.

Tutti: We found a duckway last night.
Frutti: What's a duckway?
Tutti: Oh, about five pounds.

Flip: What is the difference between a sigh, a car, and a jackass?
Flop: I give up.
Flip: A sigh is "Oh, dear!" A car is too dear.
Flop: And what is a jackass?
Flip: You, dear.

Tip: My doctor told me to exercise with dumbbells.
Top: So?
Tip: Will you join me in the gym?

12 Peculiar Parents

Father: Now, Junior, be good while I'm away.
Junior: Okay, Pop, I'll be good for a quarter.
Father: Why, son, when I was your age, I was good for nothing.

Mother: Do you like moving pictures?
Son: I sure do, Mom.
Mother: Good! Then how about helping me carry down some
       pictures from the attic?

Englishman: Sir! I'll have you know my father is an English peer
      (pier).
American: That's nothing. My father is an American doc (dock).

Neighbor: I heard your child bawling last night.
Parent: Yes, and after four bawls he got his base warmed.

First Kid: How do you know your mother wants to get rid of you?

Second Kid: Why else would she pack a road map with my lunch every day?

Mama Gnu to Papa Gnu:

"I want you to punish our little one. He's been bad all day!"

"No," replied Papa Gnu. "I won't punish him. You will have to paddle your own Gnu."

Lou: My mother thinks I'm too thin.

Ella: What gave you that idea?

Lou: She is always saying she can see right through me.

Junior: Father made a mistake this morning and ate soap flakes instead of corn flakes.

Sister: Was he angry?

Junior: He was so angry he foamed at the mouth.

A proud father was never tired of telling how smart his son Arthur was. "Arthur could recite the Gettysburg Address when he was ten years old. Lincoln didn't say it until he was fifty."

Adam and his son Cain were once walking in the fields when the boy asked: "Who was that lady I saw you out with last night?" Adam replied: "That wasn't night, that was Eve."

The little boy was riding the elevator of a tall office building with his mother and father. He tugged at his father's coat and when his father bent over, the little boy whispered in his ear.

The father frowned and shook his head. The little boy tugged at his father's coat and whispered the same thing again.

"No," said his father.

When the little boy tugged his father's coat for the third time, his father lost his patience and said sharply: "I don't care how Superman does it! We're going up this way!"

Suzie: Mom, where are the Andes?

Mother (not listening closely): How should I know? If you'd put your things away where they belong, you'd be able to find them when you need them.

A boy climbing a tree tore his trousers. His mother said, "Now, Harold, I want you to go upstairs, take off your trousers so I can fix them, and stay in your room until dinnertime."

Fifteen minutes later Harold's mother heard a noise coming from the basement. She thought Harold had disobeyed her, left his room, and was now down in the basement. She called, "You bad boy, are you down in the basement running around with your pants off?"

A man's deep voice came up from the cellar, "No, ma'am, I'm just reading the electric meter."

Sam: Father, may I have another apple?

Father: What? Another apple? Do you think they grow on trees?

Mother Lion: Junior, what are you doing?

Lion Cub: I'm chasing a hunter around a tree.

Mother Lion: How many times must I tell you not to play with your food?

Neighbor: You say your son is only four, and he can spell his name backwards as well as forwards? What is his name?

Proud Father: Otto.

Mutt: My grandfather has a wooden leg.
Jeff: That's nothing. My grandmother has a cedar chest.

"I finally made my son stop biting his nails."
"How did you manage to do that?"
"I made him wear shoes."

Mr. Smith: My son is an excellent piano player. He can even
play with his feet.
Mr. Jones: Really? How old is your son?
Mr. Smith: Fifteen.
Mr. Jones: That's nothing. My son can play with his feet, and
he's only one.

Junior: Pop, there's a man at the circus who jumps on a horse's
back, slips underneath, catches hold of its tail, and
finishes on the horse's neck!
Father: That's nothing. I did all that the first time I rode a horse.

"When are you going to fix that front fence?" the farmer's
wife asked Farmer Brown.
Farmer Brown answered, "Next week, when our son
comes home from college."
"But what does our son know about fixing a fence?" the
farmer's wife asked.
"He ought to know a lot. He wrote me that he was taking
fencing lessons."

Father: If you don't stop playing that saxophone, I'll go crazy!
Son: Too late, Pop, I stopped an hour ago.

Ernie: My grandfather was touched on the shoulder with a
sword by Queen Victoria and made a knight.
Bernie: That's nothing. My grandfather was touched on the
head with a tomahawk by an Indian and made an angel.

Father: Look at all these bills! Taxes, rent, telephone, clothes,
food. The cost of everything is going up everywhere. I'd
be happy if just one thing went down.
Son: Dad, here's my report card.

"Good Grief!" cried Whistler as he saw his mother scrubbing the floor on her hands and knees. "Are you off your rocker?"

First Father: What's all that singing coming from your house?
Second Father: It's my daughter having a folk song party.
They're pulling barges on the Erie Canal, following the weaver's trade, rowing boats ashore, and hammering all over this land. But just you ask her to clean up her room!

Fred: Where's a phone? I've got to wire my father.
Ned: What's the trouble? Can't he stand up by himself?

The mother turkey was scolding her children. "You bad children, you," she said. "If your father could only see you now, he would turn over in his gravy."

Boy: Dad, what makes the lightning?
Father: I don't know.
Boy: Dad, what makes the snow white?
Father: I don't know.
Boy: Dad, you don't mind if I bother you with all these questions?
Father: Absolutely not, son. How are you ever going to learn anything if you don't ask questions?

Ghoul Friend: My, how your little ghoul has sprouted up! The last time I saw him, he was only so high.
Ghoul Mother: Yes, he certainly gruesome.

13
Sick Sick Sick

A man went to his doctor complaining about terrible neck pains, throbbing headaches, and dizzy spells. The doctor examined him and said, "I'm afraid I have some bad news for you. You have only six months to live."

The doomed man decided he would spend his remaining time on earth enjoying himself. He told his boss what he thought of him and quit his job. Then he took all his money out of the bank and bought a sports car, ten new suits, and fifteen pairs of new shoes.

Then he went to get himself a dozen tailored shirts. He went to the finest shirt shop he could find. The tailor measured him and wrote down size sixteen neck.

"Wait a minute," the man interrupted. "I always wear a size fourteen neck, and that is what I want."

"I'd be glad to do it for you, sir," the tailor replied. "However, if you wear a size fourteen neck you're going to get terrible neck pains, throbbing headaches, and dizzy spells.'"

Patient: Can a person be in love with an elephant?
Doctor: No.
Patient: Do you know anyone who wants to buy a very large
       engagement ring?

Doctor: Please breathe out three times.
Patient: Is that so you can check on my lungs?
Doctor: No, so I can clean my eyeglasses.

    A doctor was examining a sick boy in his room. He came out of the room and asked the boy's father for a screwdriver. The father quickly fetched the screwdriver and gave it to the doctor.

    The doctor went back into the sick boy's room. In a few minutes he came out again. This time he asked for a hammer and chisel.

    The father rushed out and got the tools and the doctor went back into the boy's room.

    In a few minutes, he came out again.

    The father could stand it no longer and pleaded, "For goodness sake, Doctor, what's wrong with my son?"

    "I haven't had a chance to examine him yet," the doctor replied. "I can't get my medicine bag open."

Teacher: I excused you last week from school, Willie, because
      you said your aunt was dying. I saw her in the beauty
      parlor yesterday.
Willie: Correct. That's where she was dyeing. Now she's a
      blonde.

A vain lion wanted to find out why the other animals were not as beautiful as he.

First he asked a giraffe. The giraffe did not know. Next, the lion asked a bear. The bear had no answer. Then the lion asked a hippopotamus, and again got no answer.

Finally, the lion met a mouse. He asked the mouse, "Tell me, why aren't you as big, as strong, and as beautiful as I am?"

The mouse looked up at the lion and said, "Well, I've been sick."

Mother: Junior, why on earth did you swallow the money I gave you?
Junior: Because you said it was my lunch money.

"Was I brought here to die?" asked the first Australian as he opened his eyes in the hospital.

"No," answered the second Australian. "You were brought here yester-die."

Dit: What do you want to take for your cold?
Dot: I don't know. What'll you give me?"

A cowboy boasted to the sheriff that he had the best horse in the world.

"I was riding him through a lonely stretch of the country, when he stumbled over a rock. I fell from the saddle and broke my leg.

"Don't tell me," the sheriff said, "that the horse reset your leg!"

"Nope. But he grabbed me by the belt, dragged me home, and galloped five miles to fetch the doctor."

"I'm glad everything worked out so well," said the sheriff.

"Not really. That dumb horse fetched a horse doctor!"

Wise man says:
    An apple a day keeps the doctor away—if aimed right.

Jack: Say, Jill, how did you get that swelling on your nose?
Jill: I bent down to smell a brose in my garden.
Jack: Not brose, Jill, rose. There's no "B" in rose.
Jill: There was in this one.

Doctor: Your cough sounds much better today.
Patient: It should. I practiced all night.

Dit: What are you doing for your cold?
Dot: Nothing.
Dit: Why not?
Dot: Why should I? What's it doing for me?

Patient: Doctor, I understand that you are the greatest expert in the world for the cure of baldness. If you cure me, I'll give you anything you ask.
Doctor (after examining patient): I have some good news and some bad news. First for the bad news: I can't grow any more hair on your head. Now for the good news: I can shrink your head to fit the hair you've got.

Little Boy: My father beats me up every morning.
Little Girl: How terrible!
Little Boy: Yes, he gets up at seven and I get up at eight.

Doctor: What seems to be the problem?
Patient: I eat dates.
Doctor: What's wrong with that?
Patient: Off calendars?

Dit: What is the best way to prevent diseases caused by biting insects?
Dot: Don't bite any.

Biff: My cousin swallowed a frog.
Boff: Did it make him sick?
Biff: Sick! He's liable to croak any minute!

Psychiatrists tell us that one out of four people is mentally ill. So check your friends—if three of them seem to be all right, you're the one.

Wise man says:
    Anyone who goes to a psychiatrist ought to have his head examined.

Mother to child:
    "If you fall from that tree and break both legs, don't you come running to me."

One day a man passed by a farm and saw a beautiful horse. Hoping to buy the animal, he said to the farmer:

"I think your horse looks pretty good, so I'll give you five hundred dollars for him."

"He doesn't look so good, and he's not for sale," the farmer said.

The man insisted, "I think he looks just fine and I'll up the price to one thousand dollars."

"He doesn't look so good," the farmer said, "but if you want him that much, he's yours."

The next day the man came back raging mad. He went up to the farmer and screamed, "You sold me a blind horse. You cheated me!"

The farmer calmly replied, "I told you he didn't look so good, didn't I?"

Nit: I want a choo choo for Christmas.
Wit: A what?
Nit: A choo choo. A CHOO CHOO!
Wit: Coming down with a cold?

Dit: I see your arm's in a sling.
Dot: Yes, I get all the breaks.

Doctor: What seems to be the trouble?
Patient: I swallowed a clock last week.
Doctor: Good grief, this is serious! Why didn't you come to me
      sooner?
Patient: I didn't want to alarm anybody.

Flip: What was that terrible noise I heard before?
Flop: My sister fell down a flight of stairs.
Flip: Cellar?
Flop: No, I think she can be fixed.

Patient: Lately I've had the feeling that everyone wants to take
    advantage of me.
Doctor. That's nonsense.
Patient: Really? Thank you very much, Doctor. I feel so much
    better now. How much do I owe you?
Doctor: How much have you got?

Customer: Is your water supply healthy?
Waiter: Yes, sir, we use only well water.

Three Basic Rules for Dental Care:
1. See your dentist at regular intervals.
2. Brush your teeth after every meal.
3. Watch out for showers at the drinking fountain.

Biology Teacher: Do you know that you have sixty thousand miles of blood vessels in your body?
Pupil: No wonder I have tired blood.

Sign in a health food store:

CLOSED ON ACCOUNT OF SICKNESS!

Nurse: Doctor, there is an invisible man in the waiting room.
Doctor: Tell him I can't see him.

Roger: First I got appendicitis, then tonsillitis, followed by
      pneumonia. It was climaxed with neuritis. They finished
      me off with hypodermics and innoculation.
Dodger: How dreadful!
Roger: You can say that again. I thought I'd never get through
      that spelling test.

Hotel Guest (phoning down to the desk for the third time): Is
      this the desk clerk?
Clerk: Yes, it is. This is the third time you've called. What's
      biting you?
Hotel Guest: That's what I'd like to know.

Mutt: How did you break your arm?
Jeff: I followed my doctor's prescription.
Mutt: How could you break your arm by doing that?
Jeff: The prescription blew out of the window—and I followed
      it.

Biff: How's your nose?
Boff: Shut up!
Biff: So's mine—must be the cold weather.

     Have you heard about the amazing new discovery? It's a
pill that's half aspirin and half glue—for people who have
splitting headaches.

Flip: I'd like to tell you a joke about the measles, but I'd better not.

Flop: Why not?

Flip: You know how those things spread.

Health Hint:

Brush your teeth regularly with an electric toothbrush— and see your electrician twice a year.

Ernie: I just swallowed a bone.

Bernie: Are you choking?

Ernie: No, I'm serious.

Ding: I woke up this morning feeling awful. My head was spinning, and everything went around and around.

Dong: You must have slept like a top.

A teacher came into the classroom and noticed a girl sitting with her feet in the aisle and chewing gum.

"Eloise," said the teacher, "take that gum out of your mouth and put your feet in this instant!"

Flip: I went to the eye doctor because I saw spots in front of my eyes. He gave me glasses.

Flop: Did the glasses help?

Flip: Yes, indeed! Now I can see the spots much better.

Ted: I saw a doctor today about my poor memory.

Ned: What did he do?

Ted: He made me pay in advance.

Jekyll: Did you hear what happened to the scientist who mixed poison ivy with a four-leaf clover?
Hyde: What happened?
Jekyll: He ended up with a rash of good luck.

Jekyll: I just had my appendix removed.
Hyde: Have a scar?
Jekyll: No, thanks, I don't smoke.

First Smoker: I see you smoke the same brand of cigarettes as I do.
Second Smoker: Yes, but I don't save the coupons on the back. Do you?
First Smoker: Of course. How do you think I got my artificial lung?

Witch doctor to sick native:
"Drink this potion of ground bat wing, lizard tail, alligator scale, and hawk feather. If that doesn't work, take two aspirins twice a day."

"Other than that, Mrs. Lincoln, how did you like the play?"

14
Silly Questions—
Silly Answers

Mutt: Do you sleep on your left side or on your right side?
Jeff: I sleep on both sides. All of me goes to sleep at once.

Ernie: Are you a light sleeper?
Bernie: No, I sleep in the dark.

Customer: Do you have pig's feet?
Waiter: Yes, I do.
Customer: That's too bad. If you wear shoes, no one will notice.

Customer: Do you have frog's legs?
Waiter: No. It's a painful corn that makes me walk this way.

Lem: Is this the other side of the street?

Clem: No, it's over there.

Lem: That's weird. The fellow over there said it was over here.

Teacher: Horace, what was George Washington noted for?

Horace: His memory.

Teacher: What makes you say that?

Horace: They erected a monument to it, didn't they?

Teacher: George, what is a vacuum?

George: I can't think of it just now, but I've got it in my head.

Teacher: Lucy, what kind of leather makes the best shoes?

Lucy: I don't know, but banana peels make the best slippers.

Tommy: Teacher, would you punish me for something I didn't do?

Teacher: Of course not.

Tommy: Good, because I didn't do my homework.

Knick: What does coincidence mean?

Knack: Funny, I was going to ask you that same question.

What if William Toomey had a brother named Socket?

Did you hear about the silly kid who wanted to get his typewriter fixed because the "O" was upside down?

Silly: What is the best way to clean a tuba?

Sillier: With a tuba toothpaste.

Guest: I'd like a room for this evening.
Hotel Clerk: Single?
Guest: Yes, but I'm engaged to be married.

Monster to Pharmacistr: I would like some rat poison.
Pharmacist: Shall I wrap it up, or would you like to drink it
    here?

Little Boy: Daddy, when were you in Egypt?
Father: Egypt? I never was in Egypt.
Little Boy: Then where did you get my Mummy?

Customer: Do you serve crabs here?
Waiter: We serve everyone. Sit right down.

Customer: What is this insect in my soup?
Waiter: I wish you wouldn't ask me, sir, I don't know one bug
from another.

Customer: Waiter, there is a bug in the bottom of my teacup.
What does this mean?
Waiter: How should I know? If you want your fortune told, go
see a fortune teller.

"Excuse me, sir, are you reading that newspaper you're
sitting on?"

Ike: How can one person make so many mistakes in a single
day?
Mike: I get up early.

Silly: I'm thirsty.
Sillier: I'm Friday. Come over Saturday, and we'll have a
sundae.

Nit: If six-foot-tall Anna Story married Robert Short, what would
happen?
Wit: It would be one way of making a long story short.

Ike: Did you hear about the cross-eyed teacher?
Mike: No, what about her?
Ike: She had no control over her pupils.

Farmer: Young man, what are you doing in my tree?
Young Man: Your sign says "Keep off the Grass."

Fiddle: What would you do if you were carried out to sea on an
        iceberg?
Faddle: Keep cool until rescued.

Knock-Knock!
—Who's there?
A little kid who can't reach the bell.

Ned: I've played the piano for years—on and off.
Fred: Slippery stool?

Nit: What do you think of artificial respiration?
Wit: Me, I'd rather have the real thing.

Mother: Johnny, why did you kick your little brother in the
        stomach?
Johnny: It was his own fault, Mom. He turned around.

Dim: Did you know there is a star called Dog Star?
Wit: Are you Sirius?

Hotel Clerk: Sir, before going to your room, would you mind
        wiping the mud off your shoes?
Hillbilly: What shoes?

Teacher: What comes after the letter "A," Johnny?
Johnny: The rest of them.

Customer: Could I have a glass of water, please?
Waiter: To drink?
Customer: No, I do a high diving act.

He: Would you like to see me walk into that lion's cage and put
    my head in his mouth?
She: Yes.
He: And I thought you were a friend of mine!

Nit: How did you find the weather when you were on vacation?
Wit: It was easy. I went outside, and there it was.

Bus Passenger: I'd like a ticket to New York, please.
Ticket Seller: Do you wish to go by Buffalo?
Bus Passenger: Don't be funny! I want to go by bus.

Nita: What do you think of Red China?
Rita: It all depends on the color of the tablecloth.

Judge: Have you ever been up before me?
Accused: I don't know. What time do you get up?

Wife: There was a man here to see you this morning.
Husband: With a bill?
Wife: No, just a regular nose.

Waiter: What's wrong with the soup?
Customer: I asked for barley soup, not barely soup.

Customer: Waiter, didn't you hear me say "Well done?"
Waiter (ignoring the undercooked and still red steak): Yes, sir.
       And thank you so much for the kind words. It is so
       seldom we hear a compliment.

Ernie: Where were you born?
Bernie: In a hospital.
Ernie: How terrible! What was wrong with you?

Tutti: Do you have trouble making up your mind?
Frutti: Well, yes and no.

Guest: Can you give me a room and a bath?
Room Clerk: I can give you a room, but you'll have to take your
       own bath.

Doctor: Have your eyes been checked lately?
Patient: No, they've always been plain brown.

Tramp: Could you give me a bite?
Woman: I don't do that sort of thing myself, but if you'll wait a
       moment I'll call the dog.

Dit: Where were you born?
Dot: England.
Dit: What part?
Dot: All of me, silly.

Tom: What is the difference between an elephant and a mattababy?
Jerry: What's a "mattababy?"
Tom: Nothing, dear. What's the matter with you?

Baby Ear of Corn: Mama, where did I come from?
Mama Ear of Corn: Hush, dear, the stalk brought you.

Dick: Do you feel like a cup of coffee?
Jane: Of course not. Why, do I look like one?

Waiter: Would you like your coffee black?
Customer: What other colors do you have?

Customer: Waiter, look here, is this peach or apple pie?
Waiter: Can't you tell by the taste?
Customer: No, I can't.
Waiter: Well, then, what difference does it make?

Nit: What do you get if you cross a computer and a rubber band?
Wit: I don't know what it's called, but it makes snap decisions.

Teacher: What comes after "G?"
Sam: Whiz?
Teacher: No. Let's try again. What comes after "T?"
Sam: V?
Teacher: Sam, I'll give you just one more chance. What comes after "O?"
Sam: Boy!

Igor: Why do elephants paint their toenails red?
Boris: I don't know. Why?
Igor: So they can hide in the strawberry patch.
Boris: I don't believe that.
Igor: Did you ever see an elephant in a strawberry patch?
Boris: No!
Igor: See? It works!

Lem: Is it true that an alligator won't attack you if you carry a
      flashlight?
Clem: That depends on how fast you carry it.

Igor: What has twenty feet, green eyes, and a brown body with
       a yellow stripe?
Boris: I don't know. What?
Igor: I don't know either, but it's crawling up your back.

Mutt: Fishing?
Jeff: No, drowning worms.

Silly: Why are you swimming with your socks on?
Sillier: Because the water is cold.

Tip: I wonder why traffic lights turn red?
Top: You would too if you had to stop and go in the middle of
the street.

Nit: Did you get a haircut?
Wit: No, I got all of them cut.

Silly: Does your house have a stoop?
Billy: No, it stands straight.

Nita: Don't you think I look like a slender birch?
Rita: No, you look more like a knotty pine.

Nit: Haven't I seen your face somewhere else?
Wit: I don't think so. It's always been between my ears.

Customer: My hair is coming out pretty fast. Can you give me
something to keep it in?
Barber: Here's an empty box.

Sue: How are you doing in arithmetic?
Lou: Well, I've learned to add up all the zeros, but the numbers
are still giving me a little trouble.

Tip: How can you tell the difference between ducks and geese?

Top: A duck goes "quack, quack" and a goose goes "honk, honk."

Tip: Good. Now suppose you were hunting and a flock of birds came into sight and went "honk, honk." What would you do?

Top: I'd pull over and let them pass.

Tutti: Did you ever see a cowslip under a bush?

Frutti: No, but I saw a horsefly over a hedge.

Lem: I just met someone who is so dumb he thinks a football coach has four wheels.

Clem: How many wheels does it have?

15
Careers

Nit: How's your radio working?
Wit: It isn't working, it's playing.

Boss: Please file these letters.
Secretary: Wouldn't it be easier to trim them with a pair of
    scissors?

Silly: Do you have a hard job in the rubber band factory?
Sillier: Not at all. It's a snap.

    Did you hear about the street cleaner who was fired
because he couldn't keep his mind in the gutter?

    Did you hear about the man who lost his job as an
inspector in a mattress factory? He fell awake on the job.

Customer: Are you supposed to tip the waiters here?
Waiter: Why, yes.
Customer: Then tip me. I've been waiting for two hours.

Lem: What is the best way to carve wood?
Clem: Whittle by whittle.

Nit: My doctor specializes in taking out appendixes.
Wit: I see, he makes money on the side.

Store Manager: Aren't you the boy who applied for a job two
      weeks ago?
Boy: Yes, sir.
Manager: And didn't I say I wanted an older boy?
Boy: Yes, sir. That's why I'm back here now.

Wanted:
      Person to work on Fissionable Isotope Molecular Atomic
Reactive Counters and Triple-Phase Cyclotronic Plutonium
Hydrodynamics. *No experience necessary.*

      "Now, my good man, you've applied for the job of
railroad switchman. I'm going to ask you a few questions. First,
what would you do if you saw two trains approaching each
other on the same track?"
      "I'd throw the lever and switch one onto another track."
      "And if the signals were jammed?"
      "I'd grab a red flag and run out onto the track."
      "And if the train engineer didn't see you?"
      "I'd call my little boy."
      "Your little boy? What could he do?"
      "Nothing. He just loves to watch train wrecks."

He who keeps nose to grindstone ends up with a flat face.

Flip: Do you know why the butcher put bells on his scales?
Flop: I don't know, why?
Flip: Because he wanted to jingle all the weigh.

Butcher: The lamb I got in today is excellent.
Butcher's Wife: Must you always talk chop?

Mutt: I'm learning to be a barber.
Jeff: Will it take long?
Mutt: No, I'm studying all the short cuts.

The waitress was new and she already had dropped a load of dishes that morning. When she dropped a second load, the manager called out, "More dishes?"

As the waitress picked up the broken dishes, she said, "No, sir—less!"

Joe: When did you decide to become a parachute jumper?
Moe: When the plane caught fire.

She: Are you a toe dancer?
He: Why, no.
She: Then would you please get off my toes!

Sam, a waiter who had worked in the same restaurant for many years, passed away. His wife was heartbroken with grief. She tried fortune tellers, spiritualists, magicians—anyone who might put her in touch with Sam. But nothing worked.

One day her nephew came for a visit. She explained how much she wanted to contact Sam. Her nephew thought the ghost of her husband might be haunting the restaurant in which he worked for so many years.

The wife went to the restaurant, sat down at a table, and called, "Sam, Sam, where are you?"

Miraculously, a voice replied, "Here I am."

"Sam, can you please speak louder?" she said. "I can barely hear you."

"I can't," Sam answered.

"Well, then, can you come a little closer?" his wife begged him.

"Impossible," Sam replied. "That's not my table."

"Believe me," the salesman said to the lady, "this sewing machine will pay for itself in no time."

"Good," she replied. "When it does, send it to me."

Did you hear about the umbrella salesman who saved his money for a sunny day?

Dentist: Before I fill your tooth, I'll need a drill.
Patient: What! Can't you do your job without a rehearsal?

Nit: Why did you become a printer?
Wit: I was the right type.

Joe and Moe were two moving-van men. They were on a job. Joe said, "Moe, help me lift this chest."

"Why?" Moe asked. "Did Mrs. Smith tell you to?"

"No," Joe answered.

"Then how do you know she wants it moved?"

"Because she's under it," Joe replied.

Wife to minister eyeing waiter at restaurant:

If you want angel cake, you order angel cake.

Did you hear the one about the chauffeur who was so stupid that when his boss told him to put water in the car, he put a bucket in the back seat?

Passenger: Fourth floor, please.
Elevator Operator: Here you are, son.
Passenger: How dare you call me son? You're not my father.
Elevator Operator: I brought you up, didn't I?

Two stupid carpenters were building a wall when one noticed the other picking nails out of a box, nailing some in the wall, and throwing others away. The first man thought this was rather strange and asked, "Why are you throwing those nails away?"

"Well," replied the second carpenter, "the heads are on the wrong ends of those nails."

"You dummy, you," the first carpenter shouted, "those are for the other side of the wall!"

Clothes may not make the man—but a good suit has made many a lawyer.

The cannibal chief was about to cook his captive for dinner.

"By the way," the chief asked, "what kind of work do you do?"

His captive explained that he was an assistant editor.

"In that case," the cannibal beamed, "you will soon be an editor-in-chief!"

Flip: What kind of work do you do?
Flop: I'm a janitor.
Flip: Much money in it?
Flop: I'm cleaning up!

Did you hear about the vampire who went to sea? He signed up on a blood vessel.

Did you hear about the fellow who became an astronaut? He did it because people said he was no earthly good.

Mother: I think our son is going to be an astronaut.
Father: What makes you think so?
Mother: I spoke to his teacher today. She said he is taking up space.

Reporter (to astronaut): Tell me, what is the secret of space travel?
Astronaut: Don't look down.

Tip: I used to be a newspaperman.
Top: What happened?
Tip: Someone stole my stand.

Nit: Did you hear about the undertaker who buried a body in
the wrong place?
Wit: That was a grave mistake.

First Ghost: You work for a spiritualist, I hear.
Second Ghost: Yes, I do.
First Ghost: Is he any good?
Second Ghost: I would say medium.

Tutti: Is it true that the workers in the U.S. Mint have too much
work to do?
Frutti: Yes, and they're threatening to go on strike unless they
make less money.

Lem: Why so sad, Clem?
Clem: I lost my job as an elevator operator.
Lem: How come?
Clem: I couldn't learn the route.

Ding: I was in the army for three years.
Dong: Did you get a commission?
Ding: No, a straight salary.

Worker: Aren't you ashamed to give me such a poultry
paycheck?
Boss: You mean paltry.
Worker: No, I mean poultry. It's chicken feed.

The bus was packed. When the man tried to get on, the people already in the bus refused to let him inside.

"It's too crowded, there isn't any more room!" they shouted.

"But you've got to let me on," the man pleaded.

"Why should we? Who do you think you are, someone special?" they shouted.

"No," he pleaded, "I'm just the driver."

Moe: He must be in the watch business.
Joe: Whatever gave you that idea?
Moe: Whenever I work, he watches.

Joe: That dentist is an artist.
Moe: An artist?
Joe: Yes, you should see him draw teeth.

Wise man says:
The secret of success is getting ahead—but not a big one.

Monkey Business

Junior: Mom, how much am I worth?
Mother: To me, dear, you are worth all the money in the world.
Junior: In that case, can I have a quarter?

Banker: You can't open an account with this kind of money. These are wooden nickels!
Lumberjack: That's all right. I only want to open a shavings account.

Biff: Lend me ten dollars.
Boff: I can't spare it.
Biff: All right, lend me ten dollars and give me five dollars now. Then I'll owe you five dollars, and you'll owe me five dollars, and we'll call it square.

Ike: Lend me fifty dollars.
Mike: I only have forty.
Ike: Well, then, let me have the forty, and you can owe me the other ten.

Customer: Waiter, this food gives me heartburn.
Waiter: What did you expect—sunburn?

Book Club Selections

How to Lead a Parade by Marcia Long
Exercise for Pleasure by Charlie Haws
American Patriotic Songs by Orlando D. Free and
Homer D. Brave
Monster Making as a Hobby by Frank N. Stine
Arithmetic Simplified by Lois Carmen Denominator
Favorite Breakfast Recipes by Hammond Ecks
I Was an Avon Lady by Belle Ringer
How to Apologize by Thayer Thorry
Guide to Justice by Delores Clear
What's Up, Doc? by Howie Dewin
Stories from the Insane Asylum by I. M. Nutty

Shopper: What is the price of hamburger meat?
Butcher: Ninety cents a pound.
Shopper: Ninety cents a pound! But the store down the street
sells it for sixty cents a pound.
Butcher: Why don't you go there to shop?
Shopper: I did, but they are out of it.
Butcher: Well, when I am out of hamburger, I sell it for forty
cents a pound.

The country needed more money, so it opened a new
mint which operates from 7 P.M. to midnight. This makes it the
world's largest after-dinner mint.

Knight: I bought this suit here two weeks ago and it looks rusty already.

Armor Maker: Well, I said it would wear like iron, didn't I?

A pretty girl came into a dress shop and asked the salesclerk if she could try on the dress in the window.

"I wish you would," the salesclerk said. "It should be good for business."

Snip: I went window shopping today.
Snap: Did you get anything?
Snip: Yes, I bought four windows.

Dit: Where did Larry go?

Dot: He's round in front.

Dit: I know what he looks like, I just wanted to know where he
went.

A woman opened her refrigerator door and found a rabbit
inside.

"What are you doing in my refrigerator?" she asked.

"Isn't this a Westinghouse?" the rabbit wanted to know.

"Yes," said the woman.

"Well," replied the rabbit, "I'm westing."

Sign in a real estate office:
    LOTS FOR LITTLE!

Real Estate Agent: Here is a house without a flaw.
Customer: My goodness, what do you walk on?

Dit: Speaking of inflation, have you any idea of the price of
        feather pillows these days?
Dot: Not really.
Dit: Why, even down is up.

Tip: A man sold me the Nile River.
Top: Egypt you.

Policeman: Hey, you! You're crossing the street when the light
        says, "Don't Walk."
Pedestrian: Sorry, Officer, I thought that was an ad for the bus
        company.

Nit: How did you manage to pass the geometry test without
        studying?
Wit: I knew all the angles.

Teacher: Where is your pencil, Harold?
Harold: I ain't got none.
Teacher: How many times have I told you not to say that,
        Harold? Now listen: I do not have a pencil, you do not
        have a pencil, they do not have a pencil . . . Now,
        Harold, do you understand?
Harold: Not really. What happened to all the pencils?

A gorilla walked up to a soda fountain and ordered a chocolate ice cream soda. The man behind the counter was amazed to hear the gorilla speak, but he brought the ice cream soda anyway.

The gorilla finished the ice cream soda and handed the man a ten dollar bill. The man did not believe the gorilla knew anything about money, so he only gave back one dollar in change.

"Hope you enjoyed the soda," he said to the gorilla. "We don't get too many gorillas coming in here."

"At nine dollars a soda," said the gorilla, "it's no wonder."

"So, you run a duck farm," said the city visitor. "Is business picking up?"

"No, picking down," replied the farmer.

The farmer came into the bank and asked the guard who arranged for loans.

"I'm sorry, sir," the guard told him, "but the loan arranger is out to lunch."

"All right," the farmer said, "can I speak to Tonto?"

Sign at a butcher shop:

HONEST SCALES—NO TWO WEIGHS ABOUT IT.

Sign in funeral parlor:

SATISFACTION GUARANTEED OR YOUR MUMMY BACK!

Sign on a travel agency window:

PLEASE GO AWAY!

Sign in a canary cage in a pet shop:

FOR SALE—CHEEP!

Sign at a tire store:

WE SKID YOU NOT.

Have you heard about the new Christmas gift item? It's a combination record player and air conditioner—for people who like to play it cool.

Sign at a tailor shop:

>WE'LL CLEAN FOR YOU. WE'LL PRESS FOR YOU.
>WE'LL EVEN DYE FOR YOU!

Sign in a shoe store window:

>COME IN AND HAVE A FIT.

Angry Buyer: This car won't go up hills and you said it was a fine machine.

Auto Dealer: I said, "On the level, it's a fine machine."

Client: I'll give you five hundred dollars if you do the worrying for me.

Lawyer: Fine. Now where is the five hundred dollars?

Client: That is your first worry.

ADVERTISEMENT:

>Wanted: Hotel Workers. Only inn-experienced need apply.

Sign on a garbage truck:

>SATISFACTION GUARANTEED—OR DOUBLE YOUR
>GARBAGE BACK . . .

Lem: Down on our farm, we had a hen lay an egg six inches long.

Clem: That's nothing much. On our farm we can beat that.

Lem: How?

Clem: With an egg beater.

Customer: Waiter! This plate is wet.
Waiter: Sir, that is your soup.

Teacher: What is a conductor of electricity?
Louella: Why, er-r—
Teacher: Correct. Now tell me, Louella, what is the unit of
    electric power?
Louella: The what?
Teacher: Correct, very good.

Customer: Waiter! There is no turtle in the turtle soup.
Waiter: Of course. If you look closely you'll see that there is also
    no horse in the horseradish.

Customer: Waiter, this soup tastes funny.
Waiter: Then why aren't you laughing?

Ernie: To the right of me was a ferocious lion, on my left a tiger
    ready to spring, and in back and in front of me were
    stampeding elephants!
Bernie: How did you escape?
Ernie: I got off the merry-go-round.

17
Oldies / But Goodies

Two hillbillies were fishing. For three hours neither of them moved a muscle. Then one became restless. His companion grumbled, "That's the second time you've moved your feet in twenty minutes. Did you come here to fish or to dance?"

Iggy: Did you take a bath today?
Ziggy: Why? Is one missing?

Little Suzie: Mother, you know that vase you said had been
    handed down from generation to generation?
Mother: Yes.
Little Suzie: Well, this generation just dropped it.

Pilot: Do you wanna fly?
Co-Pilot: Sure.
Pilot: Wait a second and I'll catch one for you.

Dit: Did you hear about the delicatessen that kept bandages in
the refrigerator?
Dot: Whatever for?
Dit: For cold cuts.

Did you hear about the bank clerk who climbed a tree
because he wanted to become a branch manager?

Wise man says:
Those who eat sweets—take up two seats.

Did you hear about the mad scientist who invented a
square bathtub so it never left a ring?

"He was a Marine corporal, but they had to kick him
out."
"What for?"
"Because he was rotten to the Corps."

Juliet: Romeo, Romeo, wherefore art thou?
Romeo: Down here in the flowers. The trellis broke.

"Did you hear about the blind man who picked up a
hammer and saw?"
"No, but I heard about the dumb man who picked up a
wheel and spoke."

Nit: No one can stop time, they say.
Wit: I don't know. Why, just this morning I saw a policeman go
into a store and stop a few minutes.

Flo: What is the name of your dog?
Moe: Ginger.
Flo: Does Ginger bite?
Moe: No, but Ginger snaps.

Pitter: I have a three-season bed.
Pat: What is a three-season bed?
Pitter: One without a spring.

Mini: Did you hear about the trouble in the bakery last night?
Maxi: No, what happened?
Mini: Two stale buns tried to get fresh.

He: Do you know how to make a Venetian blind?
She: No, how?
He: Stick your finger in his eye.

Customer: Waiter, there is a fly in my soup.
Waiter: How much can a little fly drink?

Customer: Waiter, there is a fly in my soup.
Waiter: Don't worry, the spider on the bread will take care of it.

Customer: Waiter, what is this fly doing in my soup?
Waiter: It looks like the backstroke to me.

Customer: There's a fly in my soup.
Waiter: Well, it's better than having no meat at all.

Big Al: What are you doing with a pencil and paper?
Little Al: I'm writing a letter to my brother.
Big Al: But you don't know how to write.
Little Al: That's okay, my brother can't read.

Ernie: What is you pet pig's name?
Bernie: Ballpoint.
Ernie: Is that his real name?
Bernie: No, that's his pen name.

Goodenov: I woke up last night with the feeling that my watch
        was gone. So I looked for it.
Badenov: Was it gone?
Goodenov: No, but it was going.

Judge: Driving through a red light will cost you twenty-five dollars and costs, and next time you go to jail. Is that clear?

Driver: Yes, your honor. Just like a weather report—fine today, cooler tomorrow.

Mother: Who gave you the black eye?

Boy: Nobody. I had to fight for it

Mother: Now, Junior, eat your spinach. It's good for growing children.

Junior: Who wants to grow children?

Wise man says:
    Many a true word is spoken through false teeth.

Moe: Why did you bury your old car?
Joe: Well, the battery was dead, the pistons were shot, and then
    the engine died.

Father: How did you do in your exams today, Junior?
Junior: I did what George Washington did.
Father: What was that?
Junior: I went down in history.

Teacher: What does it mean when the barometer is falling?
Pupil: It means that whoever nailed it up didn't do such a good
    job.

Flip: How were the exam questions?
Flop: Easy.
Flip: Then why do you look so unhappy?
Flop: The questions didn't give me any trouble—just the
    answers.

A pet store owner was trying to sell a dog to a customer. It
was a hot day and the dog was breathing hard with his long
tongue hanging out.
    "Don't you admire his coat?" the store owner asked.
    "Coat's all right," the customer replied, "but I don't care
for the pants."

An old Indian named Short Cake died. His tribe argued about who would dig his grave. Finally, his widow settled it. She declared, "Squaw bury Short Cake."

She nodded to the minister as he passed. "Mother," asked Junior, "who was that man?"

"That is the man who married me," Mother replied.

"If that is the man who married you," asked Junior, "what's Daddy doing in our house?"

Dick: Great news! Teacher said we would have a test today, rain or shine.
Jane: What's so great about that?
Dick: It's snowing.

Ike: My brother has been playing the piano for three years.
Mike: Aren't his fingers tired?

Ned: I know someone who whistles while he works.
Ted: Is he that happy?
Ned: No, he's a traffic policeman.

Suzie: Mother, I can't go to school today.
Mother: Why not?
Suzie: I don't feel well.
Mother: Where don't you feel well?
Suzie: In school.

Teacher: Order, children, order!
Sammy: I'll have a hamburger and a coke, please.

Eke: How do you get down from a horse?

Zeke: Jump off?

Eke: Nope.

Zeke: Use a ladder?

Eke: Nope.

Zeke: Well, then, how *do* you get down from a horse?

Eke: You don't get down from a horse, you get down from a
duck.

Sports Spectacular

Game Warden: Catch any fish?

Fisherman: Did I? I took out forty this morning.

Game Warden: That's illegal. Know who I am? I'm the game warden.

Fisherman: Know who I am? I'm the biggest liar in the world.

Teacher: Now, children, I want you all to draw a ring. (Johnny draws a square.)

Teacher: Johnny, I told you to draw a ring, and you've drawn a square.

Johnny: Mine's a boxing ring.

Waiter (watching a customer dusting his plate): Pardon, sir, but may I ask what you're doing?

Customer: Sorry, force of habit. I used to be an umpire.

I finally found out why Washington was standing in that boat. Every time he sat down, somebody handed him an oar.

Sign in gym:

THE WORLD IS IN BAD SHAPE—MUST YOU BE TOO?

Dick: Did anyone laugh when you fell on the ice?
Rick: No, but the ice made some awful cracks.

Junior: I went out for the football team, Dad.
Father: Did you make it?
Junior: I think so. At the end of the practice session, the coach
        looked at me and said, "This is the end."

Sam (boasting about his hunting trip): All of a sudden I spotted a
        leopard.
Pam: You can't kid me, they come that way.

Lem: A new pitcher is coming into the baseball game.
Clem: That's a relief.

Tip: I have a chance on the baseball team
Top: I didn't know they were raffling it off.

Sue: My uncle is an umpire in a restaurant.
Lou: In a restaurant?
Sue: Yes. When someone orders pancakes, he yells, "Batter up!"

Did you hear about the man who lost the race because of his socks? They were guaranteed not to run.

Flap: My brother was doing all right until they caught up with
      him.
Jack: I didn't know your brother was a crook.
Flap: He isn't. He's an auto racer.

Ernie: The national sport in Spain is bullfighting and in England
       it's cricket.
Bernie: I'd rather play in England
Ernie: Why do you say that?
Bernie: It's easier to fight crickets.

Ned: Can you skate?
Fred: I don't know. I can't stand up long enough to find out.

A fisherman had tried several different kinds of bait without getting a single bite. In disgust he threw a handful of coins into the lake.

"Okay, wise guys," he shouted to the fish. "Go out and buy something you like!"

Ike: Did you hear about the man who went swimming in the river on Sunday? When he wanted to come on shore, he couldn't.
Mike: How come?
Ike: The banks were all closed on Sunday.

Game Warden: You can't fish without a permit.
Fisherman: Thank you just the same, but I'm doing fine with this worm.

They had to fire the baseball player. He was so kind he wouldn't even catch a fly.

Doctor: What do you dream about at night?
Patient: Baseball.
Doctor: Don't you dream about anything else?
Patient: What, and miss my turn at bat?

Did you hear about the karate expert who joined the army? The first time he saluted he nearly killed himself.

A father and his six-year-old son were watching a football game on TV.

After a particularly bad play, the father expoded: "Just look at that stupid halfback! He's fumbled three times and every time the other team has recovered the football. Why do they let a moron like that play in the game?"

The little boy thought for a moment, and offered an explanation. "Daddy," he said, "maybe it's his ball."

Teacher: Clem, who was the first to pilot an airplane at Kitty Hawk, Orville or Wilbur?
Clem: I don't know, but either one is Wright.

Igor: Why are you taking those math questions to the gym?
Boris: I have to reduce some fractions.

The two mountain climbers had reached the end of their exhausting journey. They were at the point of total collapse, but they had made it to the top. One of the mountain climbers turned to the other and said, "It almost cost us our lives to climb to the top of Mount Everest to plant the American flag, but it was worth it. Please hand me the flag."

The second mountain climber stared at him with a surprised look and said, "I thought you brought it."

Tip: Have you ever hunted bear?
Top: No, but I've gone fishing in my shorts.

Mother (to sleeping son): Johnny, wake up! It's twenty to eight.
Johnny: In whose favor?

First Hunter: Where are you going with that rifle?
Second Hunter: Hunting for alligators.
First Hunter: There are no alligators around here.
Second Hunter: I know that. If there were, I wouldn't have to
       hunt for them.

Flap: Where did you get that stuffed lion's head?
Jack: I went hunting with a club.
Flap: Wasn't it dangerous to hunt lions with only a club?
Jack: No, the club had fifty members and they all had guns.

    A hunter was deep in the jungle when he came upon a
witch doctor pounding his drum furiously.
    "What is the matter?" the hunter asked.
    "We have no water," the witch doctor replied.
    "Are you praying for rain?" the hunter asked.
    "No, I'm calling the plumber," the witch doctor
answered.

A horse applied for a job as a baseball player. The manager of the team refused to consider him at first, but the horse was persistent. He begged and begged to be given a chance, and finally the manager let him play.

The horse put on an amazing display. He easily caught every ball hit to the outfield. He pitched and struck out every man who came to bat. When his turn came to bat, he hit the first ball with such a mighty wallop that it cleared the fence and sailed right out of the ball park. Instead of running, though, the horse stayed on home plate.

"Run, you idiot!" shouted the manager. "Why don't you run?"

The horse looked at the manager and in a calm voice said, "Who ever heard of a horse running bases?"

Once a terrible golfer hit a ball onto an anthill. He went over to the anthill to hit the ball. No matter how hard he tried, all the golfer managed to do was to hit the anthill and kill many ants. At last, only two ants remained. One turned to the other and said, "If we want to stay alive, we'd better get on the ball."

First Hunter: I just met a great big bear in the woods.
Second Hunter: Did you give him both barrels?
First Hunter: Both barrels? I gave him the whole gun.

Junior: Mother, I can't find my baseball mitt.
Mother: Did you look in the car?
Junior: Where in the car?
Mother: Try the glove compartment.

Little Al: I used to be a big game hunter. Why, for years I shot lions in Alaska.
Big Al: That is impossible. There aren't any lions in Alaska.
Little Al: Of course not. I shot them all.

Nita: I used to go skiing in Florida.
Rita: That's stupid. Whoever heard of skiing in Florida?
Nita: You did. I just told you.

Father: Son, you've struck out so many times with the bases loaded in the Little League playoffs, I might have to do something I don't want to do.
Son: What's that, Dad?
Father: I may have to trade you.

Tom: Did you ever see a catfish?
Jerry: Sure!
Tom: How did it hold the rod?

At a championship high diving contest, a spectacular dive was performed to the wild applause of the audience. Then the announcer's voice came over the loudspeaker:

"Ladies and gentlemen! I have some good news and some bad news. The good news is that the judges have awarded the magnificent dive you just witnessed a perfect score. The bad news is, there was no water in the pool."

A man had been fishing all day without luck. On his way home, he stepped into a fish market and said to the clerk, "Please stand there and throw me a few of your biggest trout."

The clerk was puzzled. "Throw them to you? Whatever for?"

The man replied, "I may be a poor fisherman, but I'm no liar. I want to be able to honestly say I caught them."

Did you hear about the camper who backed into the campfire? He burned his britches behind him.

Ike: I went to a doubleheader on a hot day, but I couldn't get any soda pop to drink.
Mike: Why not?
Ike: Because the home team lost the opener.

Two detectives are standing over the dead body of a man named Juan.
First Detective: He was killed with a golf gun.
Second Detective: What is a golf gun?
First Detective: I don't know, but it sure made a hole in Juan.

Captain (boasting): This boat makes twenty knots an hour.
Passenger: How long does it take the crew to untie them?

A dentist was about to leave his office with his golf bag on his shoulder when the phone rang.

"Doctor," the caller said, "I have a terrible toothache. Can I stop by your office in a few minutes?"

"Sorry," replied the dentist, "but I have a previous appointment to fill eighteen cavities this afternoon."

Whoppers

Zeke, the owner of the local general store, was the meanest, most insulting man in town.

One day a man walked into his store with a duck under his arm. Zeke said to him: "Say, what are you doing with that pig?"

"Are you crazy!" the man replied. "Can't you see this is a duck, not a pig?"

"I wasn't talking to you," Zeke said. "I was talking to the duck."

First Kid: When you yawn, you're supposed to put your hand to your mouth.
Second Kid: What? And get bitten?

Passenger: What good is your timetable? The trains are never on time.
Conductor: And how would you know they were late if it wasn't for the timetable?

A tramp knocked at the door of an inn named "George and the Dragon."

"Could you spare a poor man a bite to eat?" he asked the woman who answered the door.

"No!" she screamed, slamming the door.

A few seconds later the tramp knocked again.

The same woman answered the door.

"Could I have a bite to eat?" said the tramp.

"Get out, you good-for-nothing!" shouted the woman. "And don't you ever come back!"

After a few minutes the tramp knocked at the door again.

The woman came to the door.

"Pardon," said the tramp, "but could I have a few words with George this time?"

Two men were riding on a train for the first time. They had brought along bananas to eat on the trip. Just as they began to peel the bananas, the train entered a dark tunnel.

"Have you eaten your banana yet?" cried the first man.

"No," replied his friend.

"Well, don't touch it!" warned the first man. "I took one bite and went blind."

Lem: Where do you bathe?
Clem: In the spring.
Lem: I didn't ask you when, I asked you where.

TV Weatherman:

The forecast for the weekend is clear and warmer with a seventy percent chance that we're wrong.

A man walking down the street saw a delivery man struggling with a large package.

"Need any help?" said the man.

"Thanks, I could use some," replied the delivery man.

They then both grabbed an end and began to struggle with the package.

After fifteen minutes, they were both exhausted.

"I guess we'd better give up," the delivery man said. "We'll never get that package on the truck."

"*On* the truck!" the man howled. "I thought you were trying to get it *off*!"

Igor: What happens if you don't pay your exorcist?
Boris: You get repossessed.

Horace: Day after day the boy and his dog went to school
      together until at last the day came when they had to part.
Morris: What happened?
Horace: The dog graduated.

Recipe for Elephant Stew
    2 medium-sized elephants
    2 rabbits
    Cut the elephants into small pieces. Add enough water for
brown gravy. Cook over fire for approximately two weeks at a
high temperature. Serves approximately 2,800 people.
    If more people are expected, add the two rabbits. But
only if necessary, because most people don't like hares in their
stew.

Nit: Don't you think I have savoir faire?
Wit: I don't think you even have carfare.

A city dweller came to a farm and saw a beautiful horse. He decided he had to have the animal. He bargained with the farmer and the farmer finally sold him the horse.

The city man jumped on the horse and said, "Giddyup!" The horse didn't budge.

The farmer explained, "This is a special kind of horse. He'll only move if you say, 'Praise the Lord.' To stop him, you have to say, "Amen.' "

Keeping this in mind, the new owner yelled, "Praise the Lord!" whereupon the horse took off with great speed. Soon horse and rider were headed for a cliff. Just in time the rider remembered to say, "Amen." The horse came to a screeching halt right at the edge of the cliff.

Relieved, the rider raised his eyes to heaven and exclaimed, "Praise the Lord!"

Their little baby was very quiet. It never spoke. They were pleased while he was still a baby, but as he grew up they began to worry because he never once made any sound. Finally, when the child was eight years old and had never spoken, he suddenly said, "Pass the salt, please!"

Shocked, his father asked, "How is it that in eight years you never once spoke a word?"

"Well, up to now everything was all right."

Lem: I went riding this morning.
Clem: Horseback?
Lem: Oh, sure. He got back two hours before I did.

A lady went into a pet shop to buy a bird. She saw one that interested her. "What kind of bird is that?" she asked the salesman.

"That is a crunchbird," he replied. "Let me show you what he can do."

"Crunchbird, my paper!" the man ordered. The bird flew down and in one gulp ate up the sheet of paper. "Crunchbird, my pencil!" The crunchbird swooped down and swallowed the pencil.

"He's wonderful!" said the lady. "I'll buy him."

The lady broght the bird home. Her husband looked at the bird and wondered what kind of bird it was. He had never seen a bird quite like it before.

"That, my dear," the wife boasted, "is a crunchbird."

The husband scratched his head. "Crunchbird?" he said. "Crunchbird, my foot!"

A young lady went to a fortune teller to have her fortune told.

"I will answer two questions for you for five dollars," the fortune teller said.

The young lady paid the fortune teller but asked, "Don't you think five dollars is a lot of money for two questions?"

"Yes, it is," answered the fortune teller. "Now what is your *second* question?"

Beggar: Pardon me, but would you give me fifty cents for a
       sandwich?
Passerby: I don't know. Let's see the sandwich.

"Tough luck," said the egg in the monastery. "Out of the frying pan into the friar."

Read in the will of a miserly millionaire:

". . . and to my dear nephew Sam, whom I promised to remember in my will, "Hi, there, Sam!' "

"Want to get close to something that has a lot of money in it?"

"Sure!"

"Go across the street and lean against the bank."

Mutt: What is that book the orchestra leader keeps looking at?
Jeff: That is the score.
Mutt: Really? Who's winning?

"You need glasses," the eye doctor said.
"I'm already wearing glasses," replied the patient.
"In that case," the doctor said, "I need glasses."

Igor: Doctor, I'm worried about my brother. He thinks he's an
elevator.
Doctor: I'll look at him. Send him up.
Igor: I can't. He doesn't stop at your floor.

Patient: I am not well, doctor.

Doctor: What seems to be the trouble?

Patient: I work like a horse, eat like a bird, and I'm as tired as a dog.

Doctor: Sounds to me like you ought to see a veterinarian, not a doctor.

The dog and his master were shown to their seats by the theater usher. When the picture was over, the dog applauded loudly. As they left the theater, the usher asked, "And did your dog enjoy the movie?"

"Very much," the dog's master replied.

"Amazing!" the usher said.

"I think so, too, especially since he didn't care for the book too much."

An Indian chief was traveling back to his reservation in New Mexico when his car broke down. Not having enough money to continue his trip, he climbed the nearest cliff and sent up smoke signals to his tribe to ask for money.

The tribe signaled back to find out what he needed it for.

Before the chief could answer, scientists from the Atomic Energy Commission exploded an atom bomb nearby. A vast column of smoke shaped like a giant mushroom filled the sky.

The tribe immediately answered back, "All right, all right, don't get so upset—we'll send the money!"

Patient: Doctor, I have a tendency to get fat in certain places. What would you recommend?

Doctor: Stay out of those places!

When my aunt heard that a milk bath is good for the skin, she asked the milkman for ten gallons.

"Do you want it pasteurized?" the milkman asked.

"No," said my aunt, "up to my knees would be fine."

On a cold, windy day in late spring, a snail started to climb a cherry tree. Some sparrows in a nearby oak laughed at the snail. Finally, one flew over and said, "Say, you nerd, don't you know there are no cherries on this tree yet?"

The snail thought a moment and said, "But there will be by the time I get there."

Ali Baba went up to the entrance of the cave and cried:
"Open Sesame!"
A voice called back:
"Says who?"

Waiter: *Hawaii*, mister. You must be *Hungary*?

Customer: Yes, *Siam*. But I can't *Rumania* here for long. *Venice* dinner being served?

Waiter: I'll *Russia* everything. What will you have? *Turkey* fried in *Greece*?

Customer: Whatever is ready. But can't *Jamaica* cook do it fast?

Waiter: *Odessa* laugh, *Juneau*. But *Alaska*.

Customer: In the meantime I'll have a cup of *Java* with a *Cuba* sugar.

Waiter: Don't be *Sicily*. *Sweden* it yourself. I'm only here to *Serbia*.

Customer: *Denmark* up my *Czech*. I don't *Bolivia* know who I am.

Waiter: I don't *Kenya* and I don't *Caribbean* about you!

Customer: *Samoa* wisecracks. What's got *India*? Do you think this arguing *Alps* business?

Waiter: You're a big *Spain* in the neck. *Abyssinia*!

Father Bear: Someone has been eating my porridge.

Mother Bear: Someone has been eating my porridge.

Baby Bear: Someone has been eating my porridge, and it's all gone!

Grandma Bear: I wish you'd all stop complaining. I haven't even served the porridge yet.

A chemist stepped up to the pharmacy counter and asked for some prepared acetylsalicylic acid.

"You mean aspirin?" asked the druggist.

"Oh, yes," answered the chemist. "I can never remember that name."

Drip: After I learned the Indian dances the members of the tribe gave me an Indian name.

Drop: What was that?

Drip: "Clumsy."

A man was taking a walk down a street when he was stopped by someone who wanted to sell a talking dog for ten dollars.

The man could not believe his ears when the dog said, "Please buy me. My owner is a mean man. He never pets me, doesn't feed me, beats me all the time. And you know, I'm really a great dog. I also was in the last war. I won the Distinguished Service Cross and the Purple Heart."

The man was amazed. "That dog really does talk. Why in the world would you want to sell him for only ten dollars?"

The owner of the dog replied, "Because I can't stand a liar."

It was the first day of school and the pupils were very excited. The school principal visited some classes and was annoyed at the commotion made by one class in particular. Unable to bear it any longer, he opened the door and burst in. He saw one boy taller than the rest who seemed to be making the most noise. He seized the lad, dragged him into the hall, and told him to stay there until he was excused.

The principal then returned to the classroom and restored order. He lectured the class for a half an hour on the importance of good behavior. He then asked, "Any questions?"

One girl timidly stood up and said, "Please, sir, may we have our teacher back?"

"Open wide," said the dentist. "Good grief! You've got the biggest cavity I've ever seen, *the biggest cavity I've ever seen*!"

"You don't have to repeat yourself," snapped the patient.

"I didn't," said the dentist. "That was an echo."

First Shark: Do you know what that funny-looking thing is with two legs swimming in the water?
Second Shark: No, but I'll bite.

A man wanted to commit suicide. To make sure he did the job, he got a bottle of poison, a rope, a gun, some gasoline, and matches.

Pouring the gasoline all over his clothing, he climbed a tree and crawled out on a branch overhanging a lake. He hung himself from the limb, drank the poison, set his clothing on fire, and then shot himself.

Alas! He missed his head, the bullet hit the rope, he fell into the water, and the water put the flames out. He swallowed so much water that the poison became harmless. Then he had to swim as hard as he could in order to save his life.

Astronauts Harry and Larry were on a spaceship circling above the earth. According to plans, Harry would leave the spaceship to go on a fifteen minute space walk, while Larry remained inside.

When Harry tried to get back in the spaceship, he found the door was locked. He knocked. There was no answer. He knocked louder. Still no answer. He pounded with all his might. Finally, he heard Larry's voice inside the spaceship, "Who's there?"

German Boy: Tell me, what is your telephone number?
German Girl: 9999999.
German Boy: All right, then don't!

Fiction Best-Seller List

1. Over the Cliff by Hugo Furst
2. Will He or Won't He? by Mae B. Sew
3. Peek-A-Boo by I. C. Hugh
4. Who Killed Cock Robin? by Howard I. Know
5. High and Dry by Rufus Leeking
6. Early One Morning by R. U. Upjohn
7. Round the Mountain by Sheila B. Cumming
8. Is It Love? by Midas Welby
9. Ten Years in the Monkey House by Bab Boone
10. Detective Stories by Watts E. Dunn

Nonfiction Best-Seller List

1. I Was a Streaker by Running Bear
2. How to Overcome Depression by M. I. Blue
3. How to Avoid Arguments by Xavier Breth
4. Button Collecting by Zipporah Broaken
5. Why You Need Insurance by Justin Case
6. How to Improve Your Looks by Celeste Chance
7. Better Target Shooting by Mr. Completely
8. How I Struck It Rich by Jack Potts
9. How to Fall out the Window by Eileen Dover
10. The Victims of Jack the Ripper by Hugh Next

20
You Asked for It

What did the scoutmaster say when his car horn was fixed?

"Beep repaired."

Tip: Please put the cord back in the plug.
Top: You mean socket.
Tip: No, I mean plug.
Top: It may be "plug" to you but it's "socket" to me.

Did you hear the one about the man who kept one hundred clocks around the house because he heard time was precious?

Did you hear the one about the girl who was so bashful she went into a closet to change her mind?

Did you hear the one about the man who moved to the city because he heard the country was at war?

Customer (to slow waiter): Have you been to the zoo?
Waiter: No, sir.
Customer: Well, you should go. You would get a kick out of
watching the snails zip by.

Iggy: So you had a nice Thanksgiving?
Ziggy: Yes, I certainly did.
Iggy: I wanted to come over for dinner, but I couldn't make it.
What did you have to be thankful for?
Ziggy: I was thankful you couldn't come over for dinner.

Captain: Have you cleared the deck and scrubbed the
portholes?
Sailor: Yes, sir, and I've even swept the horizon with the
telescope.

Flip: What is the difference between a lemon, an elephant, and a bag of cement?

Flop: I give up, what is the difference?

Flip: You can squeeze a lemon, but you can't squeeze an elephant.

Flop: What about the bag of cement?

Flip: I just threw that in to make it hard.

Joe: What are you eating?

Moe: Smart gum. It improves your mind.

Joe: Never heard of it. Where do you get it?

Moe: It's hard to find. I'll sell you some for a dollar.
(Joe bought the smart gum and chewed and chewed but nothing happened.)

Joe: Say, I've been gypped. This gum doesn't make you any smarter.

Moe: Sure it does. You're smarter already.

One day as I sat thinking, a kindly voice came to me from up above saying, "Cheer up, things could be worse."

And so I cheered up. Sure enough—things did get worse.

Wise man says:
Half a loaf is better than no time off at all.

Tip: I wish I had the money to buy an elephant.

Top: What do you want with an elephant?

Tip: Nothing, I just want the money.

"Waiter!"

"Yes, sir!"

"What is this?"

"It's bean soup, sir."

"I don't care what it's been, what is it now?"

Husband: Dear, these socks have holes in them. Will you mend them for me?

Wife: Did you get me the mink wrap I wanted?

Husband: No.

Wife: Well, if you don't give a wrap, I don't give a darn.

Igor: Did you hear about the billboard on the side of the road? It was owned by an old man called Lang.

Boris: No, I didn't.

Igor: Everybody called it Old Lang's Sign.

Did you hear about the artist who was so bad he couldn't even draw his breath?

Did you hear about the fellow who spilled some beer on the stove? Now he has foam on the range.

Did you hear about the kid who drank eight Cokes and burped Seven-Up?

Dit: Did you hear about the florist who had two children?

Dot: No, tell me.

Dit: One is a budding genius, the other a blooming idiot.

Tutti: How do you do?

Frutti: Do what?

Tutti: I mean, how do you find yourself?

Frutti: Sir, I never lose myself.

Tutti: You don't understand me. I mean, how do you feel?

Frutti: How do I feel? With my fingers, of course. Have you nothing better to do than bother me with stupid questions?

Horace: What kind of dog is that?

Morris: That's a bird dog.

Horace: Funny, I never heard him sing.

Little Kid: Show me a tough guy and I'll show you a coward.
Big Kid: Well, I'm a tough guy.
Little Kid: Well, I'm a coward.

Ned: My pet kangaroo can't wait until it's 2004.
Fred: Why is that?
Ned: It's leap year.

Judge: You've been convicted ten times of this same crime.
    Aren't you ashamed of yourself?
Accused: No, your honor. I don't believe one should be
    ashamed of one's convictions.

Customer: Waiter, I don't care for all the flies in here.
Waiter: Very well, sir. Just point out the ones you don't like, and I'll put them out.

Customer: Waiter, I'll have grits, please.
Waiter: Hominy, sir?
Customer: Oh, a couple of dozen.

Customer: Could I have a glass of water, please?
Waiter: To drink?
Customer: No, I want to rinse out a few things.

A grandmother sent her grandson a shirt for Christmas. The only trouble was that he had a size fourteen neck and the shirt was size twelve. When the grandson sent a thank you note, he wrote, "Dear Grandma, thanks a lot for the shirt. I'd write more, but I'm all choked up."

Teacher: What is the formula for water?
Jimmy: H, I J, K, L, M, N, O.
Teacher: That's not the formula I gave you.
Jimmy: You said, H to O.

Flap: Every night I take two quarters to bed with me.
Jack: Whatever for?
Flap: They are my sleeping quarters.

Moby: Have you ever seen a fish cry?
Dick: No, but I've seen a whale blubber.

Tip: I'm sorry, but I can't lend you a dollar.
Top: You're cheap.
Tip: No I'm not. I just don't believe in passing the buck.

Did you hear about the new tax for hitchers? It's a thumb tax.

Did you hear about the atomic physicist who was overworked because he had too many ions in the fire?

Did you hear the one about the man who always called a spade a spade until he tripped over one in the dark?

First Hunter: I shot one bullet and two rabbits died.
Second Hunter: That's nothing. I shot one bullet and five
        hundred frogs croaked.

He: I hope you liked the dictionary I bought for your birthday.
She: Yes, and I just can't find the words to thank you.

Last night I dreamed I was in a plane with a parachute strapped to my back. We were climbing to forty thousand feet where I was going to jump out and set a new world's record.
We got to forty thousand feet, the door opened, I took one step and plunged into space. I then pulled the rip cord and guess what? My pajamas fell down!

Tom: Did you ever see the Catskill mountains?
Jerry: No, but I've seen what cats do to mice.

All the little pigeons had left the nest and learned to fly but one. The mother pigeon said, "Son, if you don't learn to fly, I'll tow you along behind me."

"No," said the little pigeon. "I'll learn! I don't want to be pigeon-towed!"

First Kid: My father collects things. He has George Washington's watch.
Second Kid: That's nothing. My father doesn't even bother to collect things and he has an Adam's apple.

Customer: Why is this doughnut all smashed up?
Waiter: You said you wanted a cup of coffee and a doughnut
        and step on it—so I did.

Customer: I'll have a hamburger.
Waiter: With pleasure.
Customer: No, with pickles and onions.

Customer: This soup isn't fit for a pig.
Waiter: I'll take it back, sir, and bring you some that is.

Dick: I can sing "The Star-Spangled Banner" for hours.
Jane: So what? I can sing the "Stars and Stripes Forever."

Dick: How old is your brother?
Rick: He's a year old.
Dick: Huh! I've got a dog a year old and he can walk twice as
    well as your brother.
Rick: Sure, your dog has twice as many legs.

Nora: I feel like a cup of tea.
Flora: Funny, you don't look like one.
Nora: What I meant was, would you join me in a cup of tea?
Flora: Will there be enough room for both of us?
Nora: No, silly.
Flora: By the way, what hand do you use to stir your tea with?
Nora: My right hand.
Flora: Dirty thing! You should use your spoon.

Igor: What are you making?
Boris: A brilliant new invention.
Igor: Ha, ha, ha, ha!
Boris: Go ahead and laugh. They laughed at Edison, they
    laughed at Bell, they laughed at Geck.
Igor: Who's Geck?
Boris: You mean you never heard of Charles Geck?
Igor: No, what did he invent?
Boris: Nothing, but they sure laughed at him.

Customer: Have you any wild duck?
Waiter: No sir, but we can take a tame one and irritate him for
    you.

Three men went up to a haunted house because they had heard there was a fortune there.

The first man went in while the two others remained outside. He saw some money on a table and started to put the money in his pocket, when he heard a voice say, "I am the ghost of the Holy Navel, put the money back on the table!" The man ran out the back door.

The second man entered because the first took so long. He also saw the money on the table. As he started to put the money in his pocket, a strange voice said, "I am the ghost of the Holy Navel, put the money back on the table!" This man also fled out the back door.

The third man got tired of waiting, and he went inside. He saw the money. As he began to put the money in his pocket, a strange voice said, "I am the ghost of the Holy Navel, put the money back on the table!"

But instead of running away, the man said, "I am the ghost of Davy Crockett, and I'll put the money in my pocket!"

The ghost disappeared, and the man went out the front door a rich man.

Customer: I can't eat this soup.
Waiter: Sorry, sir. I'll call the manager.
Customer: Mr. Manager, I can't eat this soup.
Manager: Sorry, sir. Let me get the chef.
Customer: Chef, I can't eat this soup.
Chef: What's wrong with it?
Customer: Nothing. I just don't have a spoon.

Goodenough: Why do you think people are always taking
       advantage of Dracula?
Badenough: Because people never give a sucker an even break.

      Once upon a time there was a girl named Goldie. One
day she was walking in front of her house when she saw three
little children passing by without any clothes on. She quickly
shoved them into her house and locked the door. The name of
this story is "Goldie Locks in the Three Bears."

Ernie: I was going to tell you the story about the picture
      window, but I changed my mind.
Bernie: Oh, please tell me.
Ernie: No, I think you'd only see through it.

Pam: You should hear my new portable radio. Last night I got Mexico.

Sam: That's nothing. I just opened the window and got Chile.

Bo: The newspaper says a gunman held up a bank yesterday.

Zo: Held up a bank! I don't believe it.

Bo: Why not?

Zo: No man is that strong.

Pit: Did you hear about the formal dance in the zoo?

Pat: No, what happened?

Pit: The penguins came in tuxedos and the monkeys wore their tails.

Sherlock Holmes, that master detective, was sitting in his favorite chair smoking his pipe and reading a book when he heard a knock at the door. It was his loyal friend and assistant, Doctor Watson.

"Ah, good morning, Watson. Don't you find it a bit warm to be wearing your red flannel underwear?"

Doctor Watson was astonished by this brilliant stroke of deductive logic. "Holmes," Doctor Watson said, "how on earth did you guess I was wearing my red flannel underwear?"

"Elementary, my dear Doctor Watson, you forgot to put your pants on."

Judge: What is the prisoner charged with?
Lawyer: He is a camera enthusiast.
Judge: But you can't put a person in jail because he is crazy
    about taking pictures.
Lawyer: He doesn't take pictures, your Honor, just cameras.

Wise man says:
Life is like a shower. One wrong turn and you're in hot water.

An elegant lady dressed in furs and flashy jewels climbed on board the bus. As she handed her fare to the driver she explained, "I always have my chauffeur and my car take me wherever I wish to go. However, today the car is being repaired." Then she added with a sneer, "I haven't been on a bus in years."

The bus driver looked up at the haughty lady and said, "You can't imagine how we missed you!"

Ned: I have music in my very soul!
Fred: You're right. I did hear your shoes squeak.

Ned: I saw a man-eating shark at the aquarium.
Fred: That's nothing, I saw a man eating herring in the
    restaurant.

Bill: I know a man who drove a stagecoach and it didn't have
    any wheels.
Will: What held it up?
Bill: Bandits.

A man came into a bank and looked at the clock on the
wall. He glanced at his wristwatch and then back again at the
clock and said, "That clock is fast, isn't it?"
"Certainly," replied the teller. "It would fall down if it
weren't."

Flip: Why do you take a cane to bed with you?
Flop: In case I walk in my sleep.

Lou: How do you like the pound cake I baked?
Sue: You didn't pound it enough.

Farmer: See that pig over there? I call him "Ink."
City Man: Why do you call him that?
Farmer: Because he's always running out of the pen.

Baby Candle: Mama, I feel warm all over.
Mother Candle: That's all right, dear, it's only glowing pains.

Sign in front of a cemetery entrance:

    DUE TO A STRIKE, GRAVEDIGGING WILL
    BE DONE BY A SKELETON CREW.

    A lady brought her banged-up car to the carwash. "Can you make my car look better?" she asked.
    "Sorry, lady, we wash cars here, we don't iron them."

Customer: What's wrong with these eggs?
Waitress: Don't ask me, I only laid the table.

Nita: I just had an embarrassing experience in the kitchen.
Rita: What happened?
Nita: I opened the refrigerator and saw some Russian dressing.

Sue: I can pick up a cent with my toes.
Lou: That's nothing. My dog can do it with his nose.

Hari: What song would you sing if every person in the United States sneezed at the same time?
Kari: I give up, what song?
Hari: *"God Bless America."*

Fay and May were talking on a park bench. Said Fay, "That neighbor of yours sure is a big gossip, isn't she?"

"I'll say she is," May replied. "When she comes home from the beach, her tongue is sunburned."

Nasty Customer: Give me some cockroach powder.
Clerk: Shall I wrap it up?
Nasty Customer: No, I'll send the roaches down to eat it here.

French Chef: How do our French dishes compare with your American ones."
Tourist: They break just as easily.

Customer: This goulash tastes terrible.
Waiter: Our chef has been making goulash since before you were born.
Customer: Maybe so, but why did he save it for me?

Nit: Would you like to hear the story about the broken pencil?
Wit: No thanks, it probably has no point.

Tip: I can't understand why King Arthur had a round table.
Top: He probably didn't want to get cornered.

Wife (shaking sleeping husband): George, wake up!
George: What's the matter?
Wife: I just heard a mouse squeak.
George: What do you expect me to do, get up and oil it?

Judge: I have to let this man go free, even though I think he is
    guilty.
Attorney: How so, your honor?
Judge: The man is deaf. You know as well as I do that I can't
    convict a man without a hearing.

Wise man says:
    To err is human—to cover it up is, too.

Dit: I slept last night in a ten-foot bed.
Dot: That's a lot of bunk!

Mrs. Jones: My husband never helps me with the housework.
Mrs. Smith: My husband always does. On Monday he helped
    with the dusting. On Tuesday he helped with the
    windows. And tomorrow, he promised to mop up the
    floor with me.

Dit: I always wear sunglasses on rainy days.
Dot: Why is that?
Dit: To protect my eyes from umbrellas.

Customer: That crust on the apple pie was tough.
Waiter: That wasn't the crust, that was the paper plate.

The meal in the restaurant was awful. The diner asked to see the manager. When the manager came, the diner said, "I want to compliment you on your very clean kitchen."

"Clean kitchen?" the manager asked. "Have you seen our kitchen?"

"No," the diner replied. "But it must be clean because all the food tastes like soap."

Customer: Hey, waiter, hey!
Waiter: All right, sir, but we'll have to send out for it.

Diner: Waiter, it's been half an hour since I ordered the turtle soup.
Waiter: Yes, sir, but you know how slow turtles are.

Two boy scouts from the city were on a camping trip. The mosquitoes were so fierce, the boys had to hide under their blankets to avoid being bitten. One of them saw some lightning bugs and said to his friend, "We might as well give up. They're coming after us with flashlights."

Ned: Sardines have to be the stupidest fish in the world.
Fred: Why do you say that?
Ned: They crawl into cans, lock themselves in, and then leave the key on the outside.

First Sailor: Did you hear that the captain got married, but his wife ran away from him?
Second Sailor: Yes, I heard. He took her for a mate, but she turned out to be a skipper.

Igor: I spent ten hours over my history books last night.
Boris: You really studied, didn't you?
Igor: Who said anything about studying? The books were under
my bed.

Waiter: Oh, I am sorry I spilled water all over you.
Customer: That's perfectly all right. My suit was too large
anyhow.

Customer: Waiter, I'm in a hurry. Will the pancakes be long?
Waiter: No sir, round.

Sign on a watch repair shop:

IF IT DOESN'T TICK—TOCK TO US!

Dit: I dropped my watch.
Dot: Did it stop?
Dit: What did you expect it to do, go through the floor?

Pitter: *Hasta luego.*
Pat: What is that?
Pitter: That means "good-bye" in Spanish.
Pat: *Poison!*
Pitter: What does that mean?
Pat: That means "good-bye" in any language

Index

GIANT BOOK OF KNOCK-KNOCK JOKES

By
Ronny M. Cole
Joseph Rosenbloom

Illustrations By
Joyce Behr · Rich Garramone
Sandy Hoffman

Sterling Publishing Company, Inc.
New York

10 9 8 7 6 5 4 3

Published by Sterling Publishing Company, Inc.
387 Park Avenue South, New York, N.Y. 10016

Material in this collection was adapted from
Doctor Knock-Knock's & Nutty Knock Knocks!
© Joseph Rosenbloom
Zany Knock Knocks © Ronny M. Cole

Distributed in Canada by Sterling Publishing
c/o Canadian Manda Group, One Atlantic Avenue, Suite 105
Toronto, Ontario, Canada M6K 3E7

Distributed in Great Britain and Europe by Chris Lloyd
463 Ashley Road, Parkstone, Poole, Dorset, BH14 0AX,
United Kingdom

Distributed in Australia by Capricorn Link (Australia) Pty Ltd
P.O. Box 6651, Baulkham, Business Centre, NSW 2153, Australia

CONTENTS

Knock-Knock!

Knock–knock.
Who's there?
Aardvark.
Aardvark who?
Aardvark-um cleaner broke.
Can I borrow yours?

Knock–knock.
Who's there?
Aaron.
Aaron who?
Why Aaron you
opening the door?

Knock–knock.
Who's there?
Abbey.
Abbey who?
Abbey Birthday!

Knock–knock.
Who's there?
Abe.
Abe who?
Abe out face!

Knock–knock.
Who's there?
Abe Lincoln.
Abe Lincoln who?
Abe Lincoln (a blinkin')
yellow light means
slow down!

Knock–knock.
Who's there?
Abercrombie.
Abercrombie who?
Abercrombie (have a
crumby) time at the
party!

Knock–knock.
Who's there?
Abyssinia.
Abyssinia who?
Abyssinia at the mall!

Knock–knock.
Who's there?
Acey Ducey.
Acey Ducey who?
Acey your point, Ducey
mine?

Knock–knock.
Who's there?
Achilles.
Achilles who?
Achilles mosquitoes
with a swatter! (*Slap!*)

Knock–knock.
    Who's there?
Ada.
    Ada who?
You're Ada your mind.

Knock–knock.
    Who's there?
Adam.
    Adam who?
Adam my way–
I"m coming in!

Knock–knock.
    Who's there?
Addison.
    Addison who?
Addison no way to treat
an old friend.

Knock–knock.
    Who's there?
Afghan.
    Afghan who?
Afghan away and never
see you again.

Knock–knock.
  Who's there?
Agate.
  Agate who?
Agate you covered!

Knock–knock.
  Who's there?
Afghanistan.
  Afghanistan who?
Afghanistan out here
all night if you don't
open the door.

Knock–knock.
  Who's there?
Aiken.
  Aiken who?
Oh, my Aiken back!

Knock–knock.
  Who's there?
A la mode.
  A la mode who?
Remember the
A la mode (Alamo)!

Knock–knock.
Who's there?
Al and Edith.
Al and Edith who?
"Al and Edith love . . ."

Knock–knock.
Who's there?
Albee.
Albee who?
Albee a monkey's
uncle!

Knock–knock.
Who's there?
Alcott.
Alcott who?
Alcott the cake.
You pour the tea.

Knock–knock.
Who's there?
Alda.
Alda who?
Alda time you knew
who it was!

Knock–knock.
Who's there?
Alda and Alda.
Alda and Alda who?
I'm getting Alda and Alda
standing out here in the
cold.

Knock–knock.
Who's there?
Aldo.
Aldo who?
Aldo anything for
you.

Knock–knock.
Who's there?
Aldus.
Aldous who?
Aldous fuss over
little ol' me?

Knock–knock.
Who's there?
Aldus.
Aldous who?
Aldous knocking is
giving me a headache.

Knock–knock.
Who's there?
Aldus.
Aldus who?
Aldus talk and
no action!

Knock–knock.
Who's there?
Alec.
Alec who?
Alec-tricity. Isn't
that a shock?

Knock–knock.
Who's there?
Alex.
Alex who?
Alex-plain later.
Open the door.

Knock–knock.
Who's there?
Alex.
Alex who?
Alex the questions
around here.

Knock–knock.
Who's there?
Alfalfa.
Alfalfa who?
Alfalfa (I'll fall for) you,
if you blow in my ear.

Knock–knock.
Who's there?
Alfie.
Alfie who?
Alfie-give your rudeness—I
know you're just being
yourself.

Knock–knock.
Who's there?
Ali.
Ali who?
Ali time you
knew it was me.

Knock–knock.
Who's there?
Alistair.
Alistar who?
You uncover the pot,
Alistair the soup!

Knock–knock.
Who's there?
Alfie.
Alfie who?
Alfie you in my dreams.

Knock–knock.
Who's there?
Alice.
Alice who?
Alice fair in love
and war!

Knock–knock.
　Who's there?
Alma.
　Alma who?
The dog ate Alma
homework!

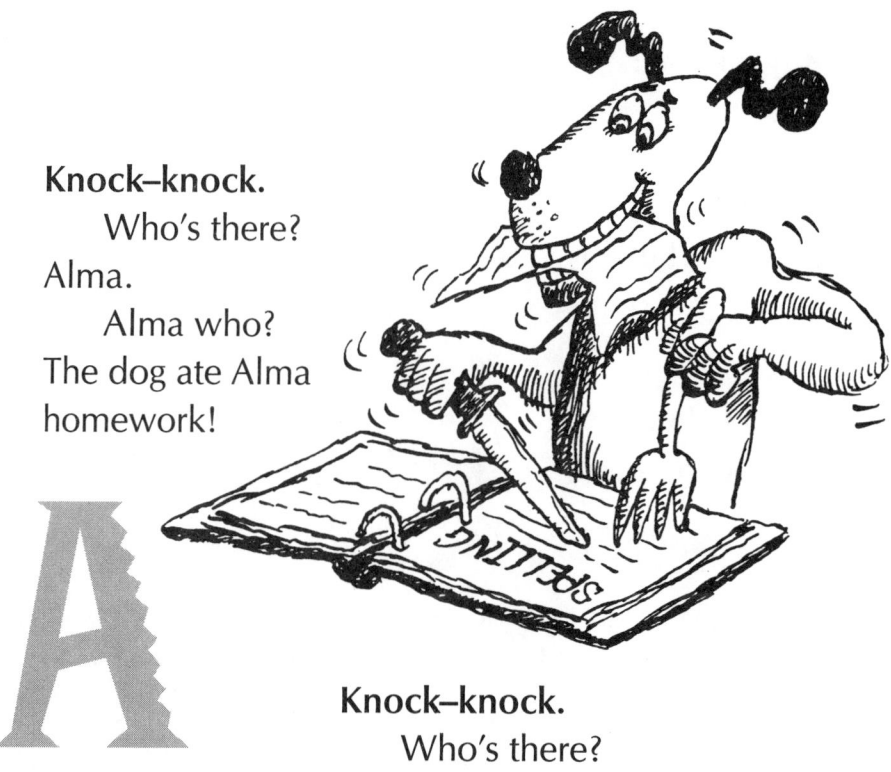

Knock–knock.
　Who's there?
Alma Gibbons.
　Alma Gibbons who?
Alma Gibbons you 24 hours
to get out of town.

Knock–knock.
　Who's there?
Aloha.
　Aloha who?
Aloha, there!

Knock–knock.
　Who's there?
Althea.
　Althea who?
Althea in jail!

Knock–knock.
　Who's there?
Altoona.
　Altoona who?
Altoona piano–you play it!

12

Knock–knock.
   Who's there?
Alva and Alma.
   Alva and Alma who?
Alva day long I spend
Alma time outside your door.

Knock–knock.
   Who's there?
Alyce.
   Alyce who?
Alyce thought you
were nuts.

Knock–knock.
   Who's there?
Amahl.
   Amahl who?
Amahl tied up,
call me later!

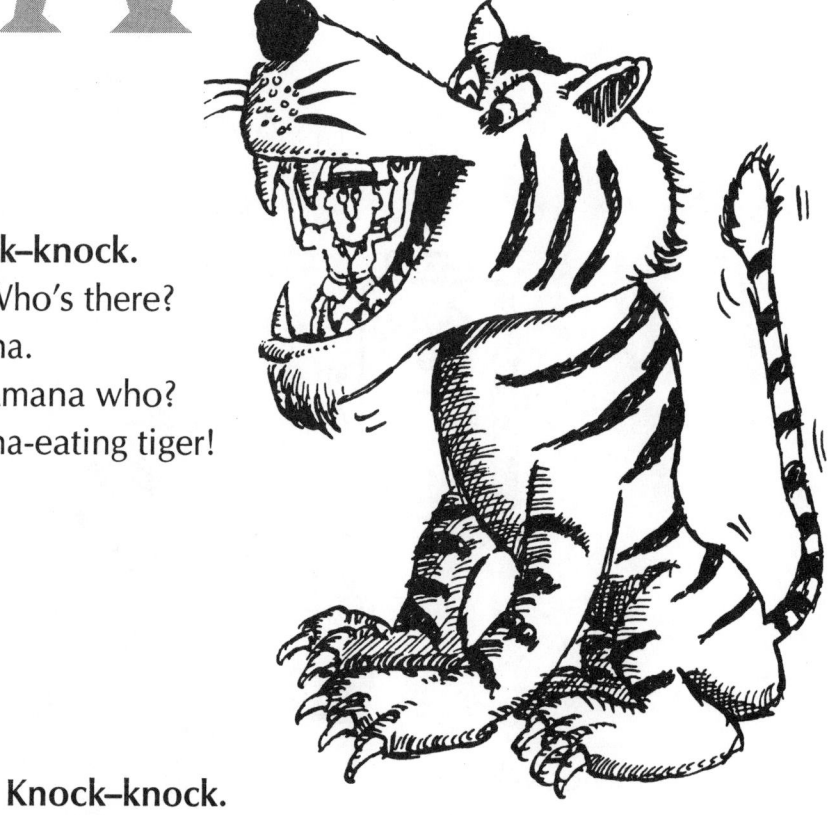

Knock–knock.
　Who's there?
Amana.
　Amana who?
Amana-eating tiger!

Knock–knock.
　Who's there?
Amanda Lynn.
　Amanda Lynn who?
Amanda Lynn player.

Knock–knock.
　Who's there?
Amarillo.
　Amarillo who?
Amarillo nice guy.

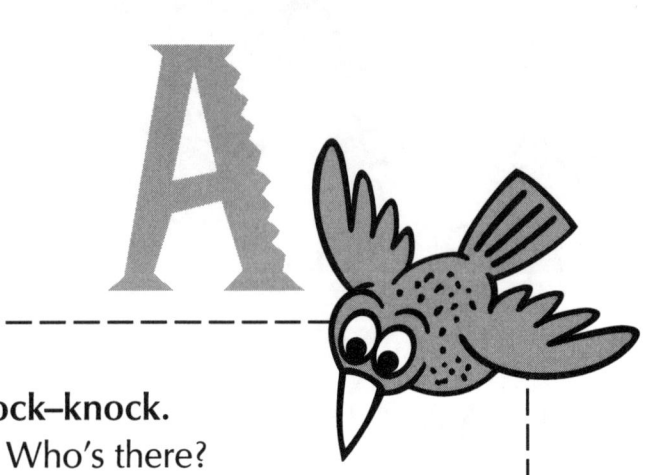

Knock–knock.
　　Who's there?
Amaryllis.
　　Amaryllis who?
Amaryllis-state agent.
Want to buy a house?

　　Knock–knock.
　　　　Who's there?
Toboggan.
　　　　Toboggan who?
Yes, but I don't like toboggan.

　　　　Knock–knock.
　　　　　　Who's there?
Arlo.
　　　　　　Arlo who?
Arlo prices can't be beat.

Knock–knock.
　Who's there?
Amateur.
　Amateur who?
Amateur service.

A

Knock–knock.
　Who's there?
Amerigo.
　Amerigo who?
Amerigo-round.

　Knock–knock.
　　Who's there?
　Vespucci.
　　Vespucci who?
　How much is Vespucci (that poochie) in the window?

Knock–knock.
Who's there?
Amen.
Amen who?
Amen hot water
again.

Knock–knock.
Who's there?
Amish.
Amish who?
Amish you sho mush!

Knock–knock.
Who's there?
Amnesia.
Amnesia who?
Oh, I see you have it, too!

A

Knock–knock.
Who's there?
Amoeba.
Amoeba who?
"Amoeba wrong,
but I think you're
wonderful . . ."

Knock–knock.
　Who's there?
Anastasia.
　Anastasia who?
Anastasia out here
in the rain.

Knock–knock.
　Who's there?
Anatol.
　Anatol who?
Anatol you what
I thought of you.

Knock–knock.
　Who's there?
Andante.
　Andante who?
I'm going to visit my
uncle Andante too.

Knock–knock.
　Who's there?
Andalusia.
　Andalusia who?
I'd like to take you
someplace Andalusia.

Knock–knock.
　Who's there?
Andy Green.
　Andy Greeen who?
"Andy Green grass grows
all around, all around . . ."

Knock–knock.
Who's there?
Angela.
Angela who?
Angela Mercy.

Knock–knock.
Who's there?
Anita.
Anita who?
Anita rest!

Knock–knock.
Who's there?
Anna Maria Alberghetti.
Anna Maria Alberghetti who?
"Anna Maria Alberghetti in a taxi, honey . . . "

Knock–knock.
Who's there?
Anna Mary.
Anna Mary who?
"Anna Mary old soul was he . . . "

Knock–knock.
Who's there?
Annapolis.
Annapolis who?
Annapolis day keeps the doctor away.

Knock–knock.
Who's there?
Annie.
Annie who?
Annie-body alive in there?

Knock–knock.
　　Who's there?
Antilles.
　　Antilles who?
Antilles open the door,
I'm gonna sit here on
your doorstep!

Dracula:	**Knock–knock.**
Victim:	Who's there?
Dracula:	A-One.
Victim:	A-One who?
Dracular:	A-One to drink your blood.

Knock–knock.
　　Who's there?
Apollo.
　　Apollo who?
Any Apollo yours
is Apollo mine.

Knock–knock.
　　Who's there?
Archer.
　　Archer who?
Archer glad to see
me?

Knock–knock.
　　Who's there?
Arcudi.
　　Arcudi who?
Arcudi little dog
can do one trick.

Knock–knock.
　Who's there?
Ariel.
　Ariel who?
You're Ariel pain
in the neck!

　　Knock–knock.
　　　Who's there?
　　Armada.
　　　Armada who?
　　Armada told us there'd
　　be days like this.

　Knock–knock.
　　Who's there?
Armand.
　　Armand who?
Armand the outside
looking inside.

　　Knock–knock.
　　　Who's there?
　　Armstrong.
　　　Armstrong who?
　　Armstrong as an ox–
　　and you have the brain
　　of one.

　　Knock–knock.
　　　Who's there?
　　Arne.
　　　Arne who?
　　Arne you going
　　to ask me in?

　　　Knock–knock.
　　　　Who's there?
　　　Arno.
　　　　Arno who?
　　　Arno kids to play
　　　with, so I'm bored.

Knock–knock.
　Who's there?
Arsenio Hall.
　Arsenio Hall who?
Arsenio Hall (I've seen
you all) over town!

Knock–knock.
　Who's there?
Artichoke.
　Artichoke who?
Artichoke on a chicken bone.

Knock–knock.
　Who's there?
Artie Fish.
　Artie Fish who?
Artie Fish-el intelligence!

Knock–knock.
   Who's there?
Aruba.
   Aruba who?
Aruba (are you the)
one in charge?

Knock–knock.
   Who's there?
Aruba.
   Aruba who?
Aruba your back,
you rub'a mine.

Knock–knock.
   Who's there?
Asbestos.
   Asbestos who?
I'm doing Asbestos I can!

Knock–knock.
   Who's there?
Ashley.
   Ashley who?
Ashley, I'm not sure . . .

Knock–knock.
   Who's there?
Ashur.
   Ashur who?
Ashur wish you'd
open this door.

Knock–knock.
    Who's there?
Asta.
    Asta who?
Asta La Veesta, baby!

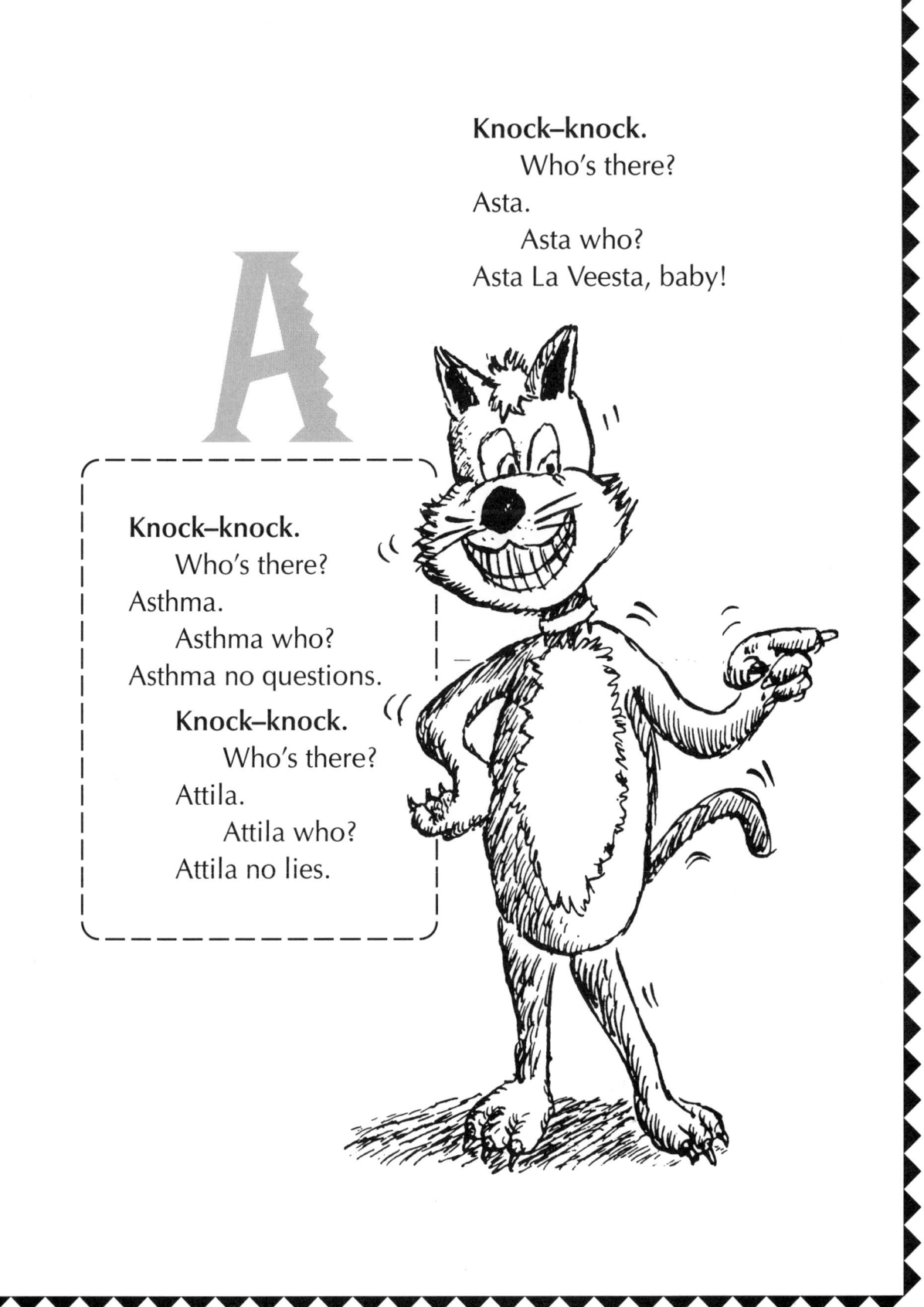

Knock–knock.
    Who's there?
Asthma.
    Asthma who?
Asthma no questions.
    Knock–knock.
        Who's there?
    Attila.
        Attila who?
    Attila no lies.

Knock–knock.
    Who's there?
Astoria.
    Astoria who?
I've got Astoria wouldn't believe!

    Knock–knock.
        Who's there?
Boris.
        Boris who?
Go ahead, Boris with another story!

Knock–knock.
    Who's there?
Attila.
    Attila who?
Attila we meet again!

Knock–knock.
    Who's there?
Atwood.
    Atwood who?
Atwood be nice if
you asked me in.

    Knock–knock.
        Who's there?
Aubrey.
        Aubrey who?
Aubrey Quiet!

Knock–knock.
  Who's there?
Auerbach.
  Auerbach who?
Please scratch
Auerbach.

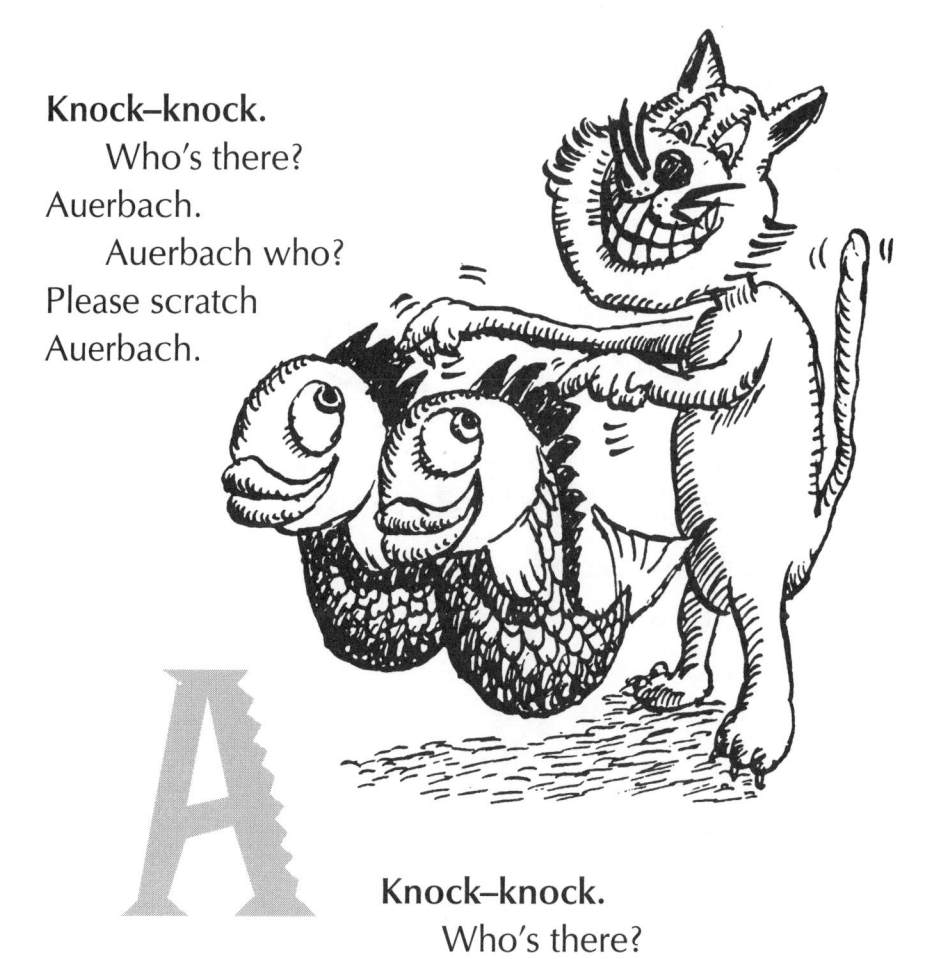

Knock–knock.
  Who's there?
Aunt Lou.
  Aunt Lou who?
Aunt Lou do you
think you are?

Knock–knock.
  Who's there?
Autumn.
  Autumn who?
You Autumn mind
your own business!

Knock–knock.
  Who's there?
Ava.
  Ava who?
Ava seen you
someplace before?

Knock–knock.
   Who's there?
Avenue.
   Avenue who?
Avenue been missing me?

Knock–knock.
   Who's there?
Avis.
   Avis who?
Avis just at the zoo
and thought about you.

    Knock–knock.
       Who's there?
    Avenue.
       Avenue who?
    Avenue heard the good news

Knock–knock.
    Who's there?
Avocado.
    Avocado who?
Avocado cold. Thad's
why I dalk dis way.

Knock–knock.
    Who's there?
Avon.
    Avon who?
Avon to be alone.

Knock-Knock!

B B B

Knock–knock.
Who's there?
Babylon.
Babylon who?
Babylon–I'm not listening anyway!

Knock–knock.
Who's there?
Babbit.
Babbit who?
Babbit and Costello!

Knock–knock.
Who's there?
Bach.
Bach who?
Bach to the future!

Knock–knock.
Who's there?
Bacilli.
Bacilli who?
Don't bacilli!

Knock–knock.
Who's there?
Baldoni.
Baldoni who?
Baldoni a little on the top.

Knock–knock.
Who's there?
Banana.
Banana who?
Banana messages
for me?

Knock–knock.
Who's there?
Barbara.
Barbara who?
"Barbara black sheep,
have you any wool . . ."

Knock–knock.
Who's there?
Barbara.
Barbara who?
The Barbara Seville.

Knock–knock.
Who's there?
Barbie.
Barbie who?
Barbie Q. Chicken.

Knock–knock.
Who's there?
B.C.
B.C. who?
B.C'ing you!

Knock–knock.
Who's there?
Bea.
Bea who?
Bea Faroni!

Knock–knock.
Who's there?
Beecher.
Beecher who?
Beecher at any game
you pick.

Knock–knock.
　Who's there?
Beehive.
　Beehive who?
Beehive yourself!

Knock–knock.
　Who's there?
Bella.
　Bella who?
Bella bottom trousers.

Knock–knock.
　Who's there?
Belladonna.
　Belladonna who?
Belladonna work, so I
had to knock.

Knock–knock.
　Who's there?
Ben and Anna.
　Ben and Anna who?
Ben and Anna split
so ice creamed.

Knock–knock.
　Who's there?
Belle Lee.
　Belle Lee who?
Belle Lee Dancer.

Knock–knock.
　Who's there?
Benny.
　Benny who?
Benny long time
no see.

31

Knock–knock.
Who's there?
Beryl.
Beryl who?
Beryl of monkeys.

Knock–knock.
Who's there?
Betty.
Betty who?
Betty B. Careful!

Knock–knock.
Who's there?
Blake.
Blake who?
Blake a leg!

Knock–knock.
Who's there?
Bertha.
Bertha who?
Bertha-day greetings.

Knock–knock.
Who's there?
Beth.
Beth who?
Beth wisheth, thweetie.

Knock–knock.
Who's there?
Betty.
Betty who?
Betty-Bye!

Knock–knock.
Who's there?
Blubber.
Blubber who?
"Blubber, come back to me . . ."

Knock–knock.
Who's there?
Bob Dwyer.
Bob Dwyer who?
Bob Dwyer out here.
Caught my pants on it.
Knock–knock.
Who's there?
Apache.
Apache who?
Apache them for
you.

B

Knock–knock.
Who's there?
Boise.
Boise who?
Boise strange!
Knock–knock.
Who's there?
Idaho.
Idaho who?
Idaho. I've seen
stranger.

Knock–knock.
  Who's there?
Boll weevil.
  Boll weevil who?
After the boll weevil
all go home.

Knock–knock.
  Who's there?
Brigham.
  Brigham who?
Brigham a present!

Knock–knock.
  Who's there?
Brighton.
  Brighton who?
Up Brighton early
just to see you.

Knock–knock.
  Who's there?
Brinckerhoff.
  Brinckerhoff who?
You Brinckerhoff the soda—
I'll bring the other half.

Knock–knock.
　Who's there?
Bruno.
　Bruno who?
Bruno who it is!

B

Knock–knock.
　Who's there?
Britches.
　Britches who?
"London Britches
falling down . . ."

Knock–knock.
　Who's there?
Buck.
　Buck who?
"Buck, buck!" I'm a chicken.

Knock–knock.
　Who's there?
Adelaide.
　Adelaide who?
Adelaide an egg.

Knock-knock.
　Who's there?
Eggs.
　Eggs who?
Eggs-tremely cold out here
in the chicken house.

Knock–knock.
    Who's there?
Buck and Ham.
      Buck and Ham who?
Buck and Ham Palace!

Knock–knock.
    Who's there?
Budapest.
      Budapest who?
You're nothing
Budapest.

Knock–knock.
    Who's there?
Butcher.
      Butcher who?
"Butcher head on my
shoulder . . ."

Knock-Knock!

Knock–knock.
    Who's there?
Caesar.
    Caesar who?
"Caesar jolly good
fellow . . ."

Knock–knock.
    Who's there?
Cain and Abel.
    Cain and Abel who?
Cain talk now–
Abel tomorrow.

Knock–knock.
    Who's there?
Cain.
    Cain who?
Cain you hear me?
Knock-Knock!

Knock–knock.
    Who's there?
Calder.
    Calder who?
Calder police–
I've been robbed!

Knock–knock.
    Who's there?
Camellia.
    Camellia who?
Camellia little closer.

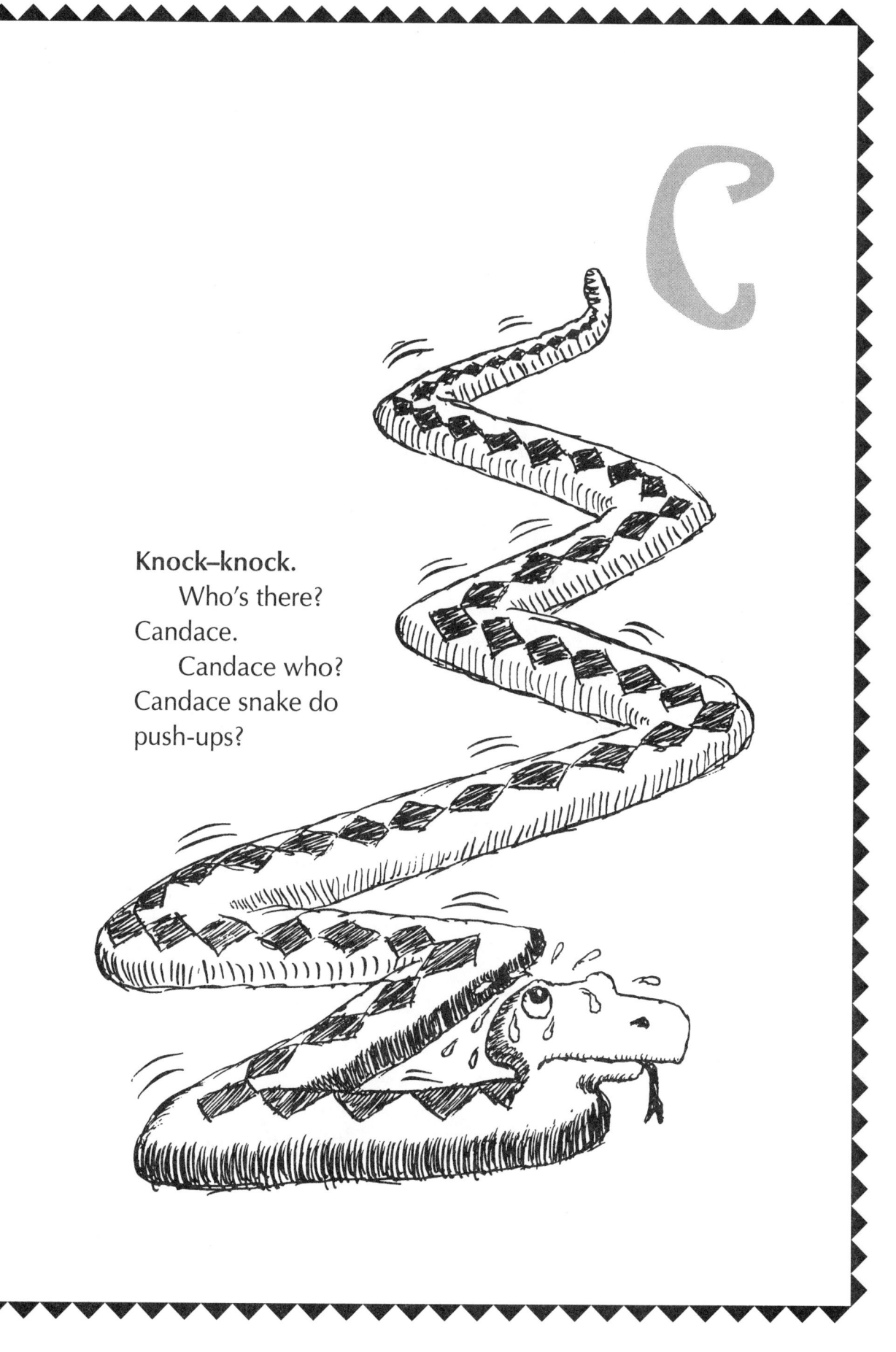

Knock–knock.
Who's there?
Candace.
Candace who?
Candace snake do
push-ups?

38

Knock–knock.
Who's there?
Cannibal.
Cannibal who?
Cannibal (can a bull) ice skate?

Knock–knock.
Who's there?
Candice.
Candice who?
Candice be love?

Knock–knock.
Who's there?
Cannibal.
Cannibal who?
Cannibal-eve you're for real!

Knock–knock.
Who's there?
Cantaloupe.
Cantaloupe who?
Cantaloupe today, maybe tomorrow . . .

Knock–knock.
Who's there?
Cantillo.
Cantillo who?
Cantillo my name, but my face will be familiar.

Knock–knock.
    Who's there?
Canoe.
    Canoe who?
Canoe please
get off my foot?

Knock–knock.
    Who's there?
Carew.
    Carew who?
The Carew of the
Love Boat.

Knock–knock.
    Who's there?
Carina.
    Carina who?
Carina ditch. Can I
use your phone?

Knock–knock.
    Who's there?
Caribbean.
    Caribbean who?
You don't Caribbean
that I'm standing out
here in a snowstorm.

Knock–knock.
    Who's there?
Carmen.
    Carmen who?
"Carmen to my parlor,"
said the spider to the fly!

C

Knock–knock.
    Who's there?
Carmen or Cohen.
    Carmen or Cohen who?
You don't know whether
you're Carmen or Cohen.

Knock–knock.
    Who's there?
Carrie.
    Carrie who?
Carrie R. pigeon.

Knock–knock.
    Who's there?
Carmencita.
    Carmencita who?
Carmencita down and take
a load off your feet.

Knock–knock.
    Who's there?
Carrie.
    Carrie who?
Carrie me inside–
I'm tired.

Knock–knock.
    Who's there?
Casanova.
    Casanova who?
Casanova (isn't over)
until the fat lady sings.

Knock–knock.
　Who's there?
Cashew.
　Cashew who?
Cashew see I'm busy?

Knock–knock.
　Who's there?
Cashew.
　Cashew who?
Cashew see it's me?

Knock–knock.
　Who's there?
Cass.
　Cass who?
Cass Toff, we're leaving!

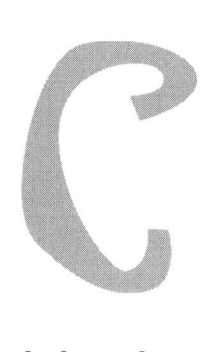

C

Knock–knock.
　Who's there?
Cassie.
　Cassie who?
Cassie Nova!
How can you
resist me?

42

C

Knock–knock.
Who's there?
Cassie.
Cassie who?
Cassie O. Watch!

Knock–knock.
Who's there?
Cassie.
Cassie who?
Cassie you know—
I've got to run!

Knock–knock.
Who's there?
Cassius.
Cassius who?
Cassius if you can!

Knock–knock.
Who's there?
Cattle Drive.
Cattle Drive who?
This Cattle (cat will)
Drive you crazy!

Knock–knock.
Who's there?
Cecilius.
Cecilius who?
Cecilius Knock–Knock
joke I ever heard.

Knock–knock.
Who's there?
Celeste.
Celeste who?
Celeste time I saw a face
like yours, I threw it a fish.

Knock–knock.
Who's there?
Celeste.
Celeste who?
Celeste you know
the better!

Knock–knock.
Who's there?
Celia.
Celia who?
Celia later, alligator!

Knock–knock.
Who's there?
Charlotta.
Charlotta who?
Charlotta fuss about
nothing.

Knock–knock.
Who's there?
Cher.
Cher who?
Cher-lock Holmes.

Knock–knock.
　　Who's there?
Cheese.
　　Cheese who?
Cheese a cute girl.

Knock–knock.
　　Who's there?
Cher.
　　Cher who?
Cher would be nice
if you opened the door!

Knock–knock.
　　Who's there?
Cherry.
　　Cherry who?
Cherry Lewis!

Knock–knock.
　　Who's there?
Chicken.
　　Chicken who?
Just Chicken out the
doorbell!

Knock–knock.
Who's there?
Chesapeake.
Chesapeake who?
Chesapeake to me and I'll tell you everything.

Knock–knock.
Who's there?
Chess game.
Chess game who?
Chess game to say goodbye.

Knock–knock.
Who's there?
Chester.
Chester who?
"Chester song at twilight . . ."

Knock–knock.
Who's there?
Chester.
Chester who?
Chester little kid!

Knock–knock.
Who's there?
Chesterfield.
Chesterfield who?
Chesterfield my leg, so I slapped him.

Knock–knock.
Who's there?
Chihuahua (pronounced Chi-*wah*-wah).
Chihuahua who?
Chihuahua buy a magazine subscription?

Knock–knock.
Who's there?
Cinnamon.
Cinnamon who?
Cinnamon-ster–
shut the door!

Knock–knock.
Who's there?
Colin.
Colin who?
Colin the doctor!
You make me sick.

Knock-knock.
Who's there?
Colleen.
Colleen who?
Colleen all cars!

Knock–knock.
    Who's there?
Cologne.
    Cologne who?
Cologne Ranger!

Knock–knock.
    Who's there?
Comma.
    Comma who?
"Comma up and
see me sometime."

Knock–knock.
    Who's there?
Collie.
    Collie who?
Collie a taxi. I'm
leaving.

Knock–knock.
    Who's there?
Concha.
    Concha who?
Concha hear me knocking?

Knock–knock.
    Who's there?
Costanza.
    Costanza who?
Costanza out here in
the rain. Open up!

Knock–knock.
    Who's there?
Crassus.
    Crassus who?
Crassus always greener
on the other side!

Knock–knock.
    Who's there?
Culligan.
    Culligan who?
I'll Culligan when you have
something intelligent to say.

Knock–knock.
    Who's there?
Cosmo.
    Cosmo who?
You Cosmo trouble
than anybody I know.

Knock–knock.
    Who's there?
Cotton.
    Cotton who?
Cotton off to a bad start!

Knock–knock.
    Who's there?
Combat.
    Combat who?
Combat tomorrow!

Knock–knock.
    Who's there?
Culver.
    Culver who?
Culver me up,
I'm freezing.

Knock–knock.
  Who's there?
Cy.
  Cy who?
Cy knew it was you, I wouldn't have bothered knocking.

Knock–knock.
  Who's there?
Czar.
  Czar who?
Czar-y about that!

Knock–knock.
  Who's there?
Apollo.
  Apollo who?
Apollo G. Accepted!

Knock-knock.
  Who's there?
Czar.
  Czar who?
Czar a doctor in the house?

Knock-Knock!

D

Knock–knock.
Who's there?
Dakar.
Dakar who?
Dakar has a flat tire!

Knock–knock.
Who's there?
Dakota.
Dakota who?
Dakota many colors.

Knock–knock.
Who's there?
Damascus.
Damascus who?
Damascus slipping off da face.

D

Knock–knock.
   Who's there?
Dandelion.
   Dandelion who?
Dandelion around out here,
but open the door anyway.

Knock–knock.
   Who's there?
Danielle.
   Danielle who?
Danielle at me, I heard
you the first time.

Knock–knock.
   Who's there?
Dancer.
   Dancer who?
"Dancer, my friend, is
blowing in the wind . . ."

Knock–knock.
   Who's there?
Darby.
   Darby who?
Darby a lot of reasons
why I knocked.

Knock–knock.
   Who's there?
Darren.
   Darren who?
Darren you to
open the door!

Knock–knock.
    Who's there?
Darth Vader.
    Darth Vader who?
Darth Vader cookie crumbles.

Knock–knock.
Who's there?
Darwin.
Darwin who?
I'll be Darwin
(there when)
you open the door.

Knock–knock.
Who's there?
Daryl.
Daryl who?
"Daryl never ever
be another you . . ."

Knock–knock.
Who's there?
Data.
Data who?
Data new hairdo or
did you just walk
through a car wash?

Knock–knock.
Who's there?
Datsun.
Datsun who?
Datsun old joke.

Knock–knock.
  Who's there?
Daughter.
  Daughter who?
Daughter-door salesman!

Knock–knock.
  Who's there?
Dawn.
  Dawn who?
Dawn do anything
I wouldn't do.

Knock–knock.
  Who's there?
Deanna.
  Deanna who?
"Till Deanna time . . ."

Knock–knock.
  Who's there?
Deanne.
  Deanne who?
I'm Deanne-sir to
your prayers!

Knock–knock.
  Who's there?
Dee Wallace.
  Dee wallace who?
"Dee Wallace came
tumbling down!"

Knock–knock.
    Who's there?
Deluxe.
    Deluxe who?
Deluxe Ness Monster.

Knock–knock.
    Who's there?
Demand.
    Demand who?
Demand from U.N.C.L.E.

Knock–knock.
    Who's there?
Denis.
    Denis who?
Denis anyone?

D

Knock–knock.
Who's there?
Dennis.
Dennis who?
Dennis says I've got a cavity.

Knock–knock.
Who's there?
Dennison.
Dennison who?
Dennison nice thing to say!

Knock–knock.
Who's there?
Denver.
Denver who?
Denver the good
old days.

Knock–knock.
Who's there?
Derision.
Derision who?
Derision room for
both of us in this town.

Knock–knock.
   Who's there?
Desi.
   Desi who?
Desi good reason why
you think the world is
against you—it is.

Knock–knock.
   Who's there?
Deuce.
   Deuce who?
Deuce something
about your dog.
He just bit me!

Knock–knock.
   Who's there?
Dexter.
   Dexter who?
"Dexter halls with
boughs of holly . . ."

Knock–knock.
   Who's there?
D-1.
   D-1 who?
I'm D-1 to watch.

Knock–knock.
   Who's there?
Diane Kilburn.
   Diane Kilburn who?
"Diane Kilburn's (the ankle bone's)
connected to the foot bone . . ."

D

Knock–knock.
   Who's there?
Diego.
   Diego who?
Diego all over your face–
what a sloppy eater!

Knock–knock.
   Who's there?
Diesel.
   Diesel who?
"Diesel man, he
played one, he
played nick-nack
on a drum . . ."

Knock–knock.
   Who's there?
Dion.
   Dion who?
Dion of thirst–can I
have a glass of water?

Knock–knock.
   Who's there?
Disease.
   Disease who?
Disease a disaster!

Knock–knock.
   Who's there?
Dishes.
   Dishes who?
Dishes the police–
open the door!

Knock–knock.
    Who's there?
Dishwasher.
    Dishwasher who?
Dishwasher last chance.

Knock–knock.
    Who's there?
Doberman pinscher.
    Doberman pinscher who?
Doberman pinscher and she
slugged him.

Knock–knock.
    Who's there?
Dizzy.
    Dizzy who?
Dizzy undertaker
know you're up?

Knock–knock.
    Who's there?
Dodson.
    Dodson who?
Dodson old Knock-Knock joke.

Knock–knock.
　Who's there?
Dog Catcher.
　Dog Catcher who?
Dog Catcher (don't count your)
chickens before they hatch!

Knock–knock.
　Who's there?
Domino.
　Domino who?
"Domino thing if you
don't have that swing . . ."

Knock–knock.
　Who's there?
Don Blaine.
　Don Blaine who?
Don Blaine (don't blame) me!

Knock–knock.
　Who's there?
Don.
　Don who?
Don mess around—
just open the door.

Knock–knock.
    Who's there?
Don Boris Witty.
    Don Boris Witty who?
Don Boris Witty details!

Knock–knock.
    Who's there?
Don Juan.
    Don Juan who?
Don Juan to go out today?

Knock–knock.
    Who's there?
Don Marcus.
    Don Marcus who?
Don Marcus absent,
we're right here!

Knock–knock.
    Who's there?
Dona Lewis.
    Dona Lewis who?
Dona Lewis (don't lose)
your temper!

Knock–knock.
　Who's there?
Donahue.
　Donahue who?
Donahue hide from
me, you rat.

Knock–knock.
　Who's there?
Donald.
　Donald who?
Donald (don't hold)
your breath!

Knock–knock.
　Who's there?
Donat.
　Donat who?
Donat be so smart.
Remember, you can
always be replaced
by a human being.

Knock–knock.
　Who's there?
Donatello.
　Donatello who?
Donatello anybody,
but I'm a werewolf.

Knock–knock.
　Who's there?
Donovan.
　Donovan who?
Donovan think about it!

Knock–knock.
    Who's there?
Donna.
    Donna who?
"Way Donna-pon the
Swanee River . . ."

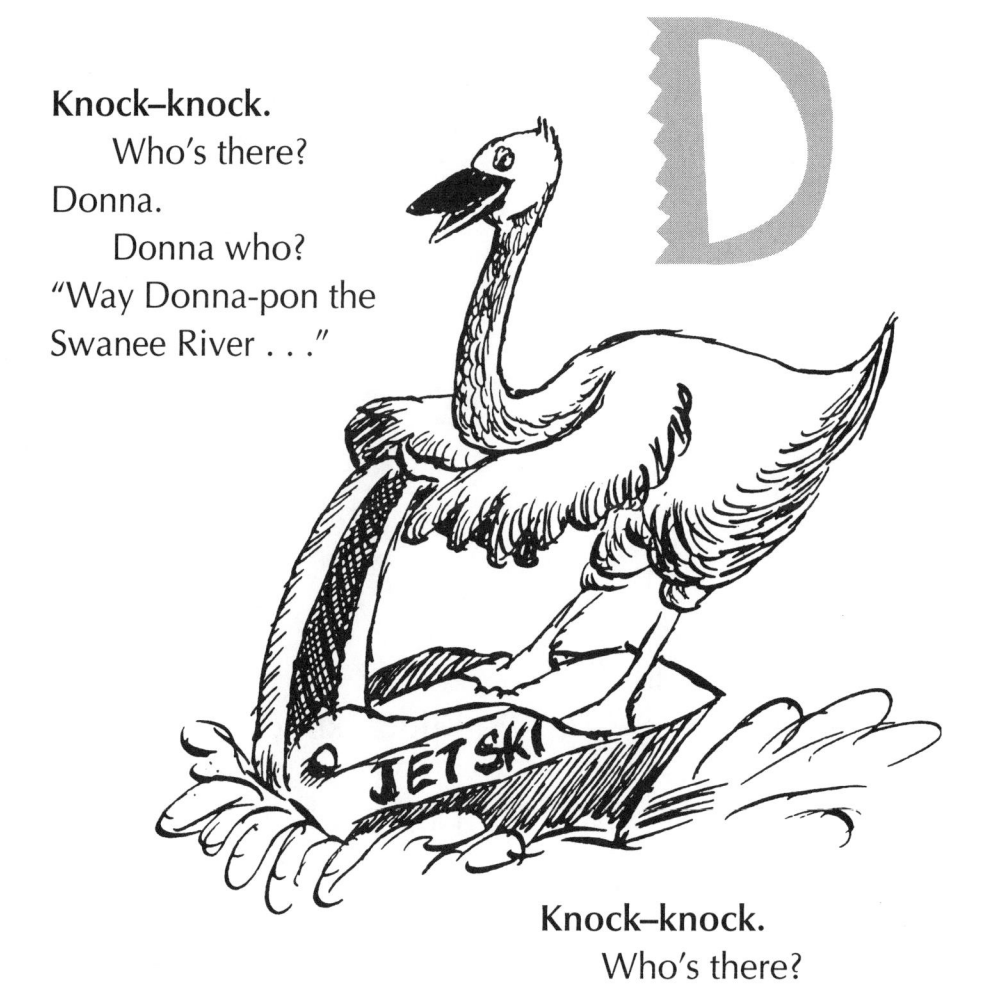

Knock–knock.
    Who's there?
Donovan.
    Donovan who?
Donovan to hear another
word out of you.

Knock–knock.
    Who's there?
Dora Belle.
    Dora Belle who?
Dora Belle is broken.
So I knocked.

Knock–knock.
 Who's there?
Doris.
 Doris who?
Doris no fool
like an old fool!

Knock–knock.
 Who's there?
Dozer.
 Dozer who?
Dozer the breaks.

Knock–knock.
 Who's there?
Doughnut.
 Doughnut who?
Doughnut be afraid–
it's only me!

Knock–knock.
Who's there?
Dragon.
Dragon who?
Dragon my name
through the mud?

Knock–knock.
Who's there?
Dragon.
Dragon who?
Quit Dragon
your tail!

Knock–knock.
Who's there?
Dresden.
Dresden who?
Dresden rags again?

Knock–knock.
  Who's there?
Dudes.
  Dudes who?
Dudes and don'ts.

Knock–knock.
  Who's there?
Duet.
  Duet who?
Duet right or don't
do it at all.

D

Knock–knock.
  Who's there?
Dunbar.
  Dunbar who?
Dunbar the door–I'll only
climb through the window..

Knock–knock.
  Who's there?
Duncan.
  Duncan who?
Duncan Donuts.

Knock–knock.
  Who's there?
Dutch.
  Dutch who?
Dutch me and I'll scream.

Knock-knock.
Who's there?
Druscilla.
Druscilla who?
Druscilla (drew a silly) picture of the teacher.

Knock-knock.
Who's there?
Mamie.
Mamie who?
She Mamie erase it.

Knock-knock.
Who's there?
Dwayne.
Dwayne who?
"Dwayne in Spain falls mainly in the plain . . ."

Knock-knock.
Who's there?
Wayne.
Wayne who?
"Wayne, Wayne go away, come again another day!"

Knock-Knock!

Knock–knock.
Who's there?
Easter.
Easter who?
Easter anybody home?

Knock–knock.
Who's there?
Eaton.
Eaton who?
Eaton out of the
garbage again?

Knock–knock.
Who's there?
Ed Rather.
Ed Rather who?
Ed Rather be sailing!

Knock–knock.
Who's there?
Edward B.
Edward B. who?
Edward B. nice if you
made like a bee and
buzzed off.

Knock–knock.
Who's there?
Efficient.
Efficient who?
Efficient my old pal!

Knock–knock.
　　Who's there?
Effie.
　　Effie who?
Effie-thing I have
is yours.

Knock–knock.
　　Who's there?
Egypt.
　　Egypt who?
Egypt you when he sold
you that busted doorbell.

Knock–knock.
Who's there?
Eiffel Tower.
Eiffel Tower who?
Eiffel (I feel) Towerable!

Knock–knock.
Who's there?
Elaine.
Elaine who?
Elaine down to take a nap.

Knock–knock.
Who's there?
Ma Belle.
Ma Belle who?
Ma Belle E. aches.

Knock–knock.
Who's there?
Cara Mia.
Cara Mia who?
Cara Mia to the doctor!

Knock–knock.
 Who's there?
Eiffel.
 Eiffel who?
Eiffel down and hurt
my knee.
 Knock–knock.
 Who's there?
Antony.
 Antony who?
Antony still hurts.

Knock–knock.
 Who's there?
Eileen Dunn.
 Eileen Dunn who?
Eileen Dunn the bell
and it broke.

Knock–knock.
 Who's there?
Eisenhower.
 Eisenhower who?
Eisenhower late–sorry!

E

Knock–knock.
 Who's there?
Elia.
 Elia who?
Elia wake at night
thinking about you.

Knock–knock.
Who's there?
Ella Mann.
Ella Mann who?
Ella Mann-tary, my
dear Watson.

Knock–knock.
Who's there?
Elke.
Elke who?
"Elke seltzer . . .
Plop, plop,
fizz, fizz . . ."

Knock–knock.
Who's there?
Ella.
Ella who?
Ella-vator.
Doesn't that give
you a lift?

Knock–knock.
Who's there?
Ellen.
Ellen who?
Ellen-eed is love.

Knock–knock.
Who's there?
Emma.
Emma who?
Emma Nemms!

Knock–knock.
Who's there?
Emanuel.
Emanuel who?
Emanuel see turn into
a werewolf when the
moon is full.

Knock–knock.
Who's there?
Emma Lou King.
Emma Lou King who?
Emma Lou King into
my crystal ball . . .

Knock–knock.
Who's there?
Emerson.
Emerson who?
Emerson of a gun!

Knock–knock.
Who's there?
Emissary.
Emissary who?
Emissary I made you cry.

Knock–knock.
Who's there?
Encino.
Encino who?
Hear no evil, speak
no evil, Encino evil!

Knock–knock.
Who's there?
Enid Sue.
Enid Sue who?
Enid Sue like a hole
in the head!

Knock–knock.
   Who's there?
Errol
   Errol who?
Errol be a hot time in
the old town tonight!

Knock–knock.
   Who's there?
Eskimo.
   Eskimo who?
Eskimo questions–
I'll tell you no lies.

Knock–knock.
   Who's there?
Estelle.
   Estelle who?
Estelle am waiting
for you to open
this door!

Knock–knock.
   Who's there?
Ethan.
   Ethan who?
Ethan this the pits?

Knock–knock.
   Who's there?
Etta.
   Etta who?
Etta Boy!

Knock–knock.
   Who's there?
Etta May Whit.
   Etta May Whit who?
Etta May Whit- (At my wits')
send!

Knock–knock.
Who's there?
Ether.
Ether who?
Ether Bunny.

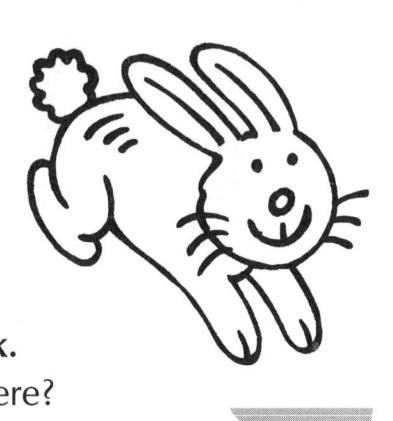

Knock–knock.
Who's there?
Cargo.
Cargo who?
Cargo "beep-beep" and
run over Ether Bunny.

Knock–knock.
Who's there?
Stella.
Stella who?
Stella 'nother Ether Bunny.

Knock–knock.
Who's there?
Consumption.
Consumption who?
Consumption be done about
all these Ether Bunnies?

Knock–knock.
Who's there?
Eubie.
Eubie who?
Eubie-lieve in law and
order—if you lay down
the law and give the order.

Knock–knock.
Who's there?
Eubie.
Eubie who?
"Eubie long to me . . ."

Knock–knock.
Who's there?
Eudora Belle.
Eudora Belle who?
Eudora Belle thing, you!

Knock–knock.
Who's there?
Eureka.
Eureka who?
Eureka perfume! Who
sold it to you—a skunk?

Knock–knock.
Who's there?
Eudora.
Eudora who?
Eudora is stuck!

Knock–knock.
Who's there?
Europe.
Europe who?
Europe (you're up)
to no good!

E

Knock–knock.
Who's there?
European.
European who?
European in the
neck.

Knock–knock.
Who's there?
Evan.
Evan who?
Evan Lee coffee!

Knock–knock.
Who's there?
Evan.
Evan who?
Evan seen
anything like you
since the Rocky
Horror Show.

Knock–knock.
Who's there?
Eye Sore.
Eye Sore who?
Eye Sore them coming!

Knock–knock.
Who's there?
Ewell.
Ewell who?
Ewell catch more flies
with honey than with
vinegar!

Knock–knock.
Who's there?
Eyes.
Eyes who?
Eyes got another
Knock-Knock joke.

Knock–knock.
Who's there?
Nose.
Nose who?
I nose another
Knock-Knock joke.

Knock–knock.
Who's there?
Ears.
Ears who?
Ears another
Knock-Knock joke.

Knock–knock.
Who's there?
Chin.
Chin who?
Chin up—I'm not going to
tell any more Knock-Knock
jokes.

Knock-Knock!

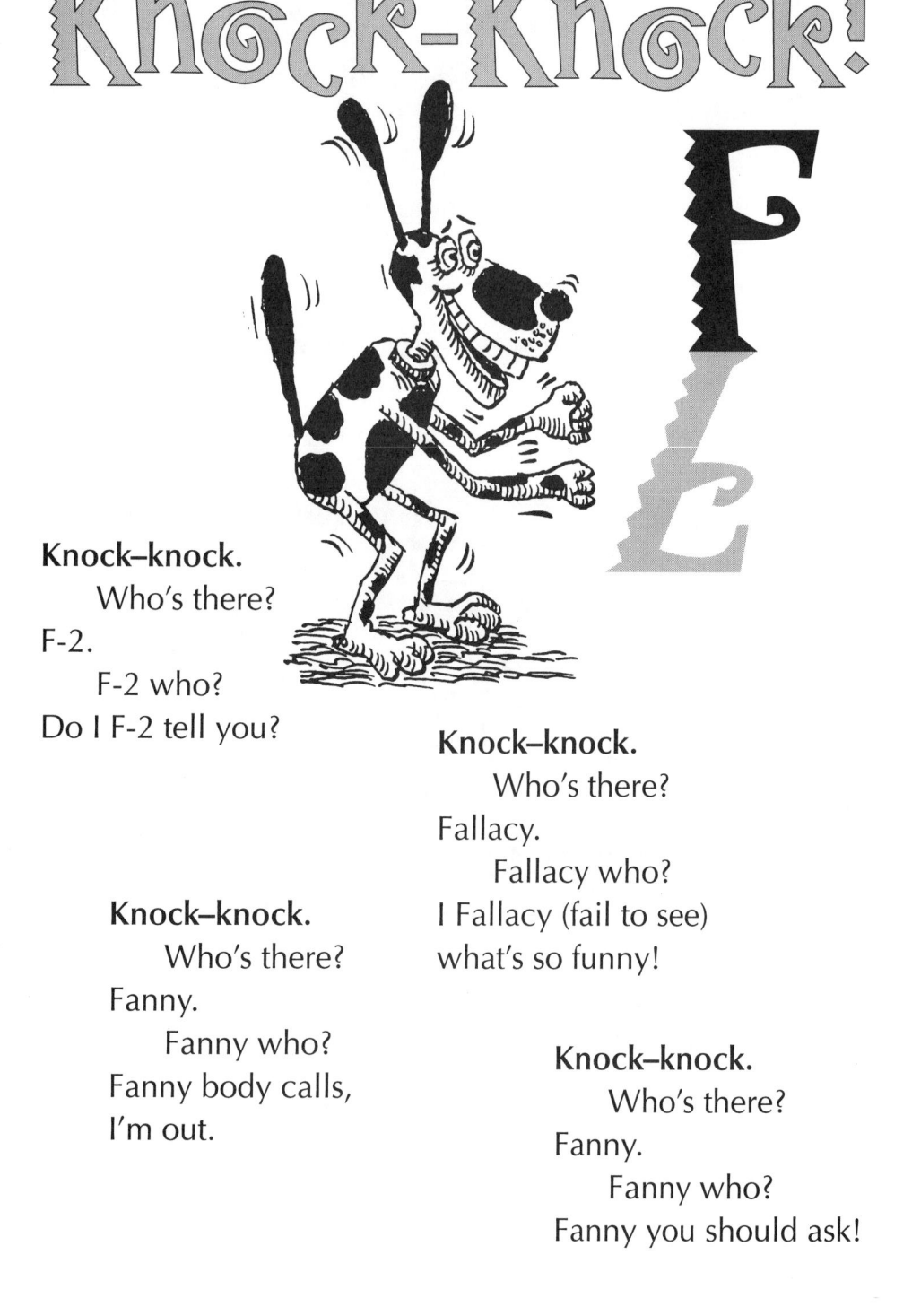

F

Knock–knock.
Who's there?
F-2.
F-2 who?
Do I F-2 tell you?

Knock–knock.
Who's there?
Fallacy.
Fallacy who?
I Fallacy (fail to see)
what's so funny!

Knock–knock.
Who's there?
Fanny.
Fanny who?
Fanny body calls,
I'm out.

Knock–knock.
Who's there?
Fanny.
Fanny who?
Fanny you should ask!

Knock–knock.
Who's there?
Far Side.
Far Side who?
As Far Side (far as I)
know, it's still me!

Knock–knock.
Who's there?
Faraday.
Faraday who?
Faraday last time,
open up!

Knock–knock.
Who's there?
Farrah.
Farrah who?
Farrah 'n wide.

Knock–knock.
Who's there?
Farrah.
Farrah who?
Farrah out, man.

Knock–knock.
Who's there?
Farris.
Farris who?
"Mirror, mirror on
the wall. Who's the
Farris one of all?"

Knock–knock.
Who's there?
Father.
Father who?
The Father the better!

Knock–knock.
Who's there?
Fatso Kay.
Fatso Kay who?
Fatso Kay with you,
Fatso Kay with me!

Knock–knock.
Who's there?
Fedora.
Fedora who?
Fedora shut, does that
mean I can't come in?

Knock–knock.
Who's there?
Felix.
Felix who?
Felix-cited all over.

Knock–knock.
Who's there?
Ferdie.
Ferdie who?
Ferdie last time,
open the door!

Knock–knock.
Who's there?
Ferrara.
Ferrara who?
"Long ago and
Ferrara-way . . ."

Knock–knock.
Who's there?
Ferris.
Ferris who?
Ferris I'm concerned,
we're through.

Knock–knock.
Who's there?
Fess.
Fess who?
Fess Aid Squad.

Knock–knock.
Who's there?
Fiddlesticks.
Fiddlesticks who?
Fiddlesticks (feet'll stick) out
if the blanket's too short.

Knock–knock.
Who's there?
Fidel.
Fidel who?
Fidel you a secret, will
you keep it to yourself?

Knock–knock.
    Who's there?
Fido.
    Fido who?
Fido away, what
will you give me?

Knock–knock.
    Who's there?
Fiendish.
    Fiendish who?
Fiendish your dinner!

Knock–knock.
    Who's there?
Fiona.
(Pronounced Fee-oh-na)
    Fiona who?
Fiona had something better
to do, do you think we'd
hang around here?

Knock–knock.
    Who's there?
Fission.
    Fission who?
Fission for compliments!

F

Knock–knock.
Who's there?
Fitzhugh.
Fitzhugh who?
If the shoe Fitzhugh
wear it!

Knock–knock.
Who's there?
Fletcher.
Fletcher who?
Fletcher self go!

Knock–knock.
Who's there?
Flaherty.
Flaherty who?
Flaherty will get
you nowhere!

Knock–knock.
    Who's there?
Fonzi.
    Fonzi who?
Fonzi meeting
you here!

Knock–knock.
    Who's there?
Florist.
    Florist who?
You can't see the
Florist for the trees!

Knock–knock.
    Who's there?
Ford.
    Ford who?
Ford-y thieves.

Knock–knock.
    Who's there?
Foreign.
    Foreign who?
"Foreign twenty
blackbirds baked
in a pie . . ."

Knock–knock.
    Who's there?
Formosa.
    Formosa who?
Formosa my life, I've
been waiting for you
to open the door!

Knock–knock.
    Who's there?
Formosa.
    Formosa who?
Formosa the day
I've had my foot stuck
in this door.

Knock–knock.
    Who's there?
Forty.
    Forty who?
Forty last time,
open up!

Knock–knock.
    Who's there?
Frank.
    Frank who?
Frank N. Stein. Aaggh!

Knock–knock.
    Who's there?
Frank Lee.
    Frank Lee who?
Frank Lee, it's none of
your business.

Knock–knock.
    Who's there?
Frank's eye.
    Frank's eye who?
Frank's eye needed that.

Knock–knock.
    Who's there?
Franz.
    Franz who?
"Franz, Romans, countrymen . . ."

Knock–knock.
    Who's there?
Franz.
    Franz who?
Franz forever!

Knock–knock.
    Who's there?
Fred.
    Fred who?
Fred I'll have to tell
you another joke.

Knock–knock.
    Who's there?
Freddie.
    Freddie who?
Freddie or not, here
I come.

Knock–knock.
    Who's there?
Freedom.
    Freedom who?
Never mind—let
freedom ring.

Knock–knock.
    Who's there?
Free Stew.
    Free Stew who?
The Free Stew-ges
(The Three Stooges).

Knock–knock.
    Who's there?
Freeze.
    Freeze who?
"Freeze a jolly
good fellow . . ."

Knock–knock.
Who's there?
Freighter.
Freighter who?
Freighter open the door?

Knock–knock.
Who's there?
Freud.
Freud who?
A-Freud you were
going to ask that.

Knock–knock.
Who's there?
Fresno.
Fresno who?
"Rudolf the Fresno
reindeer . . ."

Knock–knock.
Who's there?
Fu Manchu.
Fu Manchu who?
Fu Manchu bubble gum
the way you do.

Knock–knock.
Who's there?
Frieda.
Frieda who?
Who's a Frieda the
big bad wolf?

Knock-Knock!

G
G

Knock–knock.
    Who's there?
GM.
    GM who?
GM I rattling your cage?

Knock–knock.
Who's there?
Gallo.
Gallo who?
Gallo your dreams.

G

Knock–knock.
Who's there?
Galahad.
Galahad who?
I knew a Galahad
two left feet!

Knock–knock.
Who's there?
Garcia.
Garcia who?
Garcia (go see) the
principal.

Knock–knock.
Who's there?
Garter.
Garter who?
Garter go now!

Knock–knock.
Who's there?
Gauguin.
Gauguin who?
Gauguin, it's your turn!

Knock–knock.
Who's there?
Ghana.
Ghana who?
Not Ghana take this
anymore.

Knock–knock.
　　Who's there?
Gavin.
　　Gavin who?
Gavin you one more chance
to open the door!

Knock–knock.
　　Who's there?
Dustin.
　　Dustin who?
Dustin off the battering ram!

Knock–knock.
　　Who's there?
Germaine.
　　Germaine who?
Germaine (you're mean)
to act this way!

Knock–knock.
　　Who's there?
Gideon.
　　Gideon who?
Gideon your horse
and let's go!

Knock–knock.
　　Who's there?
Gillette.
　　Gillette who?
If Gillette me in, I
won't knock anymore.

Knock–knock.
Who's there?
Giovanni.
Giovanni who?
Giovanni come out and play?

Knock–knock.
Who's there?
Festival.
Festival who?
Festival I have to do my homework.

Knock–knock.
Who's there?
Gibbon.
Gibbon who?
Are you Gibbon me trouble?

Knock–knock.
Who's there?
Gil Diaz.
Gil Diaz who?
Gil Diaz (guilty as) charged!

Knock–knock.
Who's there?
Giuseppe.
Giuseppe who?
Giuseppe (just stepped) in something on your doorstep.
Knock–knock.
Who's there?
Houdini.
Houdini who?
Houdini that thing on your doorstep?

Knock–knock.
Who's there?
Gladwin.
Gladwin who?
Gladwin you leave town.

Knock–knock.
Who's there?
Gladys.
Gladys who?
Gladys see you.

Knock–knock.
Who's there?
G-Man.
G-Man who?
G-Man-y Crickets!

Knock–knock.
    Who's there?
Goody.
    Goody who?
"Goody-vening!" says
Count Dracula.

Knock–knock.
    Who's there?
Venom.
    Venom who?
Venom I going to get inside?

G

Knock-knock.
　　Who's there?
Goat.
　　Goat who?
Goat to your room!

Knock–knock.
　　Who's there?
Goddess.
　　Goddess who?
Goddess stop meeting
like this.

G

Knock–knock.
　　Who's there?
Goddard.
　　Goddard who?
You Goddard be kidding!
　　Knock–knock.
　　　Who's there?
Aikido.
　　　Aikido who?
Aikido you not!

Knock–knock.
Who's there?
Gopher.
Gopher who?
Gopher (go for) broke.

Knock–knock.
Who's there?
Gorilla.
Gorilla who?
Gorilla cheese sandwich.

Knock–knock.
Who's there?
Goliath.
Goliath who?
Goliath down. You're sick in the head.

Knock–knock.
Who's there?
Gordie.
Gordie who?
Gordie-rectly to jail.
Do not pass Go.
Do not collect $200.

Knock–knock.
Who's there?
Grammar.
Grammar who?
Grammar crackers.
Pretty crummy, huh?

Knock–knock.
Who's there?
Gray Z.
Gray Z. who?
Gray Z. mixed-up kid!

Knock–knock.
Who's there?
Greta.
Greta who?
You Greta my nerves.

Knock–knock.
Who's there?
Gretel.
Gretel who?
"Gretel-long little
dogie . . ."

Knock–knock.
Who's there?
Guava.
Guava who?
Guava good time!

Knock–knock.
Who's there?
Gucci.
Gucci who?
Gucci-Gucci-Goo!

G

Knock–knock.
Who's there?
Guinevere.
Guinevere who?
Guinevere going to
get together?

Knock–knock.
Who's there?
Guinness.
Guinness who?
Guinness a break!

Knock–knock.
Who's there?
Gunboat.
Gunboat who?
You're Gunboat not
forgotten.

Knock–knock.
> Who's there?

Gummy.
> Gummy who?

Gummy five!

Knock–knock.
> Who's there?

Gunnar.
> Gunnar who?

Gunnar huff and puff
and blow your house in.

Knock–knock.
> Who's there?

Gus.
> Gus who?

That's what *you're*
supposed to do.

Knock–knock.
> Who's there?

Guthrie.
> Guthrie who?

Guthrie blind mice.

Knock–knock.
> Who's there?

Gwynn N.
> Gwynn N. who?

Gwynn N. bear it!

Knock-Knock!

H

Knock–knock.
    Who's there?
Habit.
    Habit who?
Habit your own way!

Knock–knock.
    Who's there?
Hackett.
    Hackett who?
I can't Hackett–
I'm going home.

Knock–knock.
    Who's there?
Haiku.
    Haiku who?
"Haiku-d have danced
all night . . ."

H

Knock–knock.
　Who's there?
Hair combs.
　Hair combs who?
Hair Combs the judge!

Knock–knock.
　Who's there?
Halibut.
　Halibut who?
Halibut lending me
five dollars?

Knock–knock.
　Who's there?
Hallways.
　Hallways who?
Hallways knew you'd
never amount to much.

Customer: **Knock–knock.**
Waiter: Who's there?
Customer: Hammond.
Waiter: Hammond who?
Customer: Hammond eggs, please.

Knock–knock.
Who's there?
Hannah.
Hannah who?
"Hannah partridge
in a pear tree . . ."

Knock–knock.
Who's there?
Hanover.
Hanover who?
Hanover your money.

103

Knock-knock.
Who's there?
Hans.
Hans who?
Hans up! I'm a burglar.

Knock–knock.
Who's there?
Jimmy.
Jimmy who?
Jimmy your money–or else!

Knock–knock.
Who's there?
Bruce.
Bruce who?
Careful–I Bruce easily.

Knock–knock.
Who's there?
Hardy.
Hardy who?
Hardy, har, har!

Knock–knock.
Who's there?
Harley.
Harley who?
Harley ever see you around anymore.

Knock–knock.
Who's there?
Harmon.
Harmon who?
Harmon your side.

Knock–knock.
   Who's there?
Harmony.
   Harmony who?
Harmony times do I have
to knock at this door?

Knock–knock.
   Who's there?
Harold.
   Harold who?
Harold are you?

Knock–knock.
   Who's there?
Harris.
   Harris who?
Harris the world treating you?

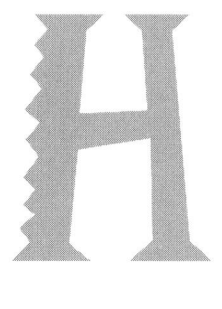

Knock–knock.
   Who's there?
Harrison.
   Harrison who?
Harrison idea–you tell the next
joke!

Knock–knock.
   Who's there?
Hartley.
   Hartley who?
This is Hartley the time to be
telling knock-knock jokes!

Knock–knock.
　Who's there?
Harv and Hugh.
　Harv and Hugh who?
Harv and Hugh (haven't you)
got a minute?

Knock–knock.
　Who's there?
Harvard.
　Harvard who?
Harvard you like a
punch in the nose?

Knock–knock.
　Who's there?
Harvey.
　Harvey who?
Harvey going to play
this game forever?

Knock–knock.
　Who's there?
Hattie.
　Hattie who?
Hattie do, you all!

Knock–knock.
　Who's there?
Hawaii.
　Hawaii who?
Hawaii doing?

Knock–knock.
　Who's there?
Healy.
　Healy who?
Healy my pain . . .

Knock–knock.
　Who's there?
Heath.
　Heath who?
"For Heath a jolly
good fellow . . ."

Knock–knock.
Who's there?
Heaven.
Heaven who?
Heaven seen you
for a long time.

Knock–knock.
Who's there?
Hedda.
Hedda who?
Hedda I win, tails
you lose!

Knock–knock.
Who's there?
Heidi.
Heidi who?
Heidi go seek.

Knock–knock.
Who's there?
Heifer.
Heifer who?
Heifer (half a) cow
is better than none.

Knock–knock.
Who's there?
Hedda.
Hedda who?
Hedda feeling you
wouldn't open the
door.

Knock–knock.
Who's there?
Heide.
Heide who?
Heide-clare war on you!

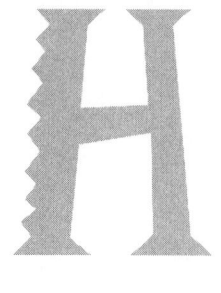

Knock–knock.
Who's there?
Hello Etta.
Hello Etta who?
"Hello Etta, gentille Alouetta . . ."

Knock–knock.
    Who's there?
Henny.
    Henny who?
Henny Penny. The sky is falling down!

Knock–knock.
    Who's there?
Izzy.
    Izzy who?
Izzy end of the world!

Knock–knock.
    Who's there?
Henrietta.
    Henrietta who?
Henrietta big dinner and got sick.

Knock–knock.
    Who's there?
Romeo and Juliet.
    Romeo and Juliet who?
Romeo and Juliet the same thing–and died.

Knock–knock.
    Who's there?
Hester.
    Hester who?
Hester any food left?

Knock–knock.
    Who's there?
Pasadena.
    Pasadena who?
Pasadena under the
door—I'm starved.

Knock–knock.
　Who's there?
Hertz.
　Hertz who?
Hertz me more than it hurts you.

　　　　Knock–knock.
　　　　　Who's there?
　　　　Hewlett.
　　　　　Hewlett who?
　　　　Hewlett you out of your cage?

Knock–knock.
　Who's there?
Heywood, Hugh and Harry.
　Heywood, Hugh and Harry who?
Heywood, Hugh Harry and open the door!

Knock–knock.
> Who's there?

Hiawatha.
> Hiawatha who?

Hiawatha very bad today.

Knock–knock.
> Who's there?

Highway cop.
> Highway cop who?

Highway cop screaming–
thinking of you.

Knock–knock.
> Who's there?

Hiram.
> Hiram who?

Hiram fine, how are you?

Knock–knock.
> Who's there?

Hiram.
> Hiram who?

Hiram glad you asked!

Knock–knock.
Who's there?
Hobbit.
Hobbit who?
Hobbit letting me in?

Knock–knock.
Who's there?
Holden.
Holden who?
Holden up everything
on account of you.

Knock–knock.
Who's there?
Hollis.
Hollis who?
Come back, Hollis
(all is) forgiven!

Knock–knock.
Who's there?
Hominy.
Hominy who?
Hominy rocks did they
have to turn up before
you crawled out?

Knock–knock.
Who's there?
Holmes.
Holmes who?
Holmes sweet home.

Knock–knock.
　Who's there?
Honda.
　Honda who?
"Home, home Honda
range . . ."

Knock–knock.
　Who's there?
Honda.
　Honda who?
Honda road again!

Knock–knock.
　Who's there?
Honeydew.
　Honeydew who?
Honeydew you think you're
ever going to open the door?

Knock–knock.
　Who's there?
Honorless.
　Honorless who?
Honorless you open this door,
I'll have to break it down!

Knock–knock.
　Who's there?
Horace.
　Horace who?
Horace I to know
you lived here?

Knock–knock.
　Who's there?
Horace.
　Horace who?
Horace of a different color!

Knock–knock.
　Who's there?
House.
　House who?
House it going?

Knock–knock.
     Who's there?
Hoodoo.
     Hoodoo who?
Hoodoo you want it to be?
     Knock–knock.
          Who's there?
San Juan.
          San Juan who?
San Juan (someone) else!

Knock–knock.
     Who's there?
Howard.
          Howard who?
Howard I know?

Knock–knock.
     Who's there?
Howard.
     Howard who?
Howard you like to crawl
back under your rock?

Knock–knock.
     Who's there?
Howell.
     Howell who?
Howell I get in if you
don't answer the door?

114

Knock–knock.
Who's there?
Hubie Maddern.
Hubie Maddern who?
Hubie Maddern a wet hen!

Knock–knock.
Who's there?
Hugh Hefner.
Hugh Hefner who?
Hugh Hefner trouble with
the doorknob again?

Knock–knock.
Who's there?
Hugo N.
Hugo N. who?
Hugo N. Crazy—
and I'm goin' home.

Knock–knock.
Who's there?
Humus.
Humus who?
Humus be sick–that
can't be your real face!

Tap–tap.
Who's there?
Hurd.
Hurd who?
Hurd my hand so I
can't knock-knock.

Knock–knock.
　Who's there?
Hutch.
　Hutch who?
Gersundheit!

Knock–knock.
　Who's there?
Huron.
　Huron who?
Huron away from
home again?

Knock–knock.
　Who's there?
Hy.
　Hy who?
Hy-oh, Silver!

Knock–knock.
　Who's there?
Hyam Alda.
　Hyam Alda who?
Hyam Alda washed up.

116

Knock-Knock!

Knock–knock.
Who's there?
I.B. Long.
I.B. Long who?
I.B. Long inside.
It's cold out here.

Knock–knock.
Who's there?
Ice Water.
Ice Water who?
My Ice Water when I
chop onions!

Knock–knock.
Who's there?
Ice cream soda.
Ice cream soda who?
Ice cream soda (I scream so the) whole world will know what a nut you are.

Knock–knock.
Who's there?
Ichabod.
Ichabod who?
Ichabod (it's a bad) night out. Can I borrow your umbrella?

Knock–knock.
Who's there?
Icon.
Icon who?
Icon live without you!

Knock–knock.
Who's there?
Ida Clair.
Ida Clair who?
Ida Clair, you're the most stubborn person!

Knock–knock.
Who's there?
Ida Klein.
Ida Klein who?
Ida Klein to answer that question!

Knock–knock.
Who's there?
Ida.
Ida who?
Ida know. Sorry.

Knock–knock.
　Who's there?
Ida.
　Ida who?
Idaho–not Ida-who!
Can't you spell?

Knock–knock.
　Who's there?
Igloo.
　Igloo who?
"Igloo knew Suzie
like I know Suzie . . ."

Knock–knock.
　Who's there?
Igor.
　Igor who?
Igor to see you again.

Knock–knock.
　Who's there?
India.
　India who?
"India good old
summertime . . ."

Knock–knock.
　Who's there?
Ina Claire.
　Ina Claire who?
"Ina Claire day, you
can see forever . . ."

Knock–knock.
Who's there?
Indonesia.
Indonesia who?
I look at you and I get weak Indonesia.

Knock–knock.
Who's there?
Indochina.
Indochina who?
The bull Indochina shop.

Knock–knock.
Who's there?
Iodine.
Iodine who?
Iodine (I'm a dyin')
for a pizza!

Knock–knock.
Who's there?
Iona.
Iona who?
"Iona have one life to
give for my country . . ."

Knock–knock.
Who's there?
Iona.
Iona who?
"Iona have eyes
for you . . ."

Knock–knock.
Who's there?
I-one.
I-one who?
"I-one-der who's
kissing her now . . ."

Knock–knock.
Who's there?
Ira.
Ira who?
Ira-turn with another
Knock-knock joke.

Knock–knock.
Who's there?
Iris.
Iris who?
Iris you were here.

Knock–knock.
   Who's there?
Iris.
   Iris who?
Iris you were here.

Knock–knock.
   Who's there?
Iraq and Iran.
   Iraq and Iran who?
Iraq'd up the car and
Iran all the way over.

Knock–knock.
   Who's there?
Irish Stew.
   Irish Stew who?
Irish Stew would come
out and play.

Knock–knock.
   Who's there?
Isabelle.
   Isabelle who?
Isabelle broken?

Knock–knock.
   Who's there?
Isadore.
   Isadore who?
Isadore stuck?

Knock–knock.
Who's there?
Isaiah.
Isaiah who?
Isaiah there, old chap, why
don't you open the door?

Knock–knock.
Who's there?
Istanbul.
Istanbul who?
Istanbul fight over?

Knock–knock.
Who's there?
Isthmus.
Isthmus who?
Isthmus be the right place.

Knock–knock.
   Who's there?
Ivan.
   Ivan who?
Ivan infectious disease.

Knock–knock.
   Who's there?
Ivy Leaf.
   Ivy Leaf who?
Ivy Leaf you alone.

Knock–knock.
   Who's there?
Ivan.
   Ivan who?
"Ivan working on
the railroad . . ."

Knock-Knock!

J

Knock–knock.
Who's there?
Jack N.
Jack N. who?
Jack N. the Box.

Knock–knock.
Who's there?
Janet R.
Janet R. who?
Janet R. in a drum.

Knock–knock.
Who's there?
Java.
Java who?
Java lot to learn!

Knock–knock.
Who's there?
Jackal.
Jackal who?
Jackal lantern.

Knock–knock.
Who's there?
Jeff.
Jeff who?
Jeff Boy-R-Dee.

Knock–knock.
Who's there?
Jenny.
Jenny who?
Jenny'd any help
opening the door?

Knock–knock.
Who's there?
Jerome.
Jerome who?
Have it Jerome way!

Knock–knock.
Who's there?
Jess Horace.
Jess Horace who?
Jess Horace-n' around!

Knock–knock.
Who's there?
Jericho.
Jericho who?
Jericho to Disneyland?

Knock–knock.
Who's there?
Jess B.
Jess B. who?
Jess B. Cuzz!

Knock–knock.
Who's there?
Jess.
Jess who?
Jess knock it off!

Knock–knock.
Who's there?
Jess me.
Jess me who?
"Jess me and my
shadow . . ."

Knock–knock.
   Who's there?
Jess.
   Jess who?
Jess one of those things.

Knock–knock.
   Who's there?
Jason.
   Jason who?
"I'm always Jason
rainbows . . ."

Knock–knock.
   Who's there?
Jessica.
   Jessica who?
Jessica (you're sicker)
than I thought.

Knock–knock.
   Who's there?
Jester.
   Jester who?
Jester minute, pardner.

Knock–knock.
   Who's there?
Jester.
   Jester who?
Jester minute, I've got
more knock-knock jokes!

Knock–knock.
Who's there?
Jethro.
Jethro who?
Jethro (just throw)
me a few bones.

Knock–knock.
Who's there?
Jethro.
Jethro who?
Jethro the boat and
stop talking so much.

Knock–knock.
Who's there?
Jezebel.
Jezebel who?
Jezebel on the door,
but it won't ring.

Knock–knock.
Who's there?
Jewel.
Jewel who?
Jewel (you'll) remember me
after you see my face.

Knock–knock.
Who's there?
Joe King.
Joe King who?
You must be Joe King!

Knock–knock.
 Who's there?
Jock.
 Jock who?
Jock-late milk shake.

Knock–knock.
 Who's there?
Johann Sebastian Bach.
 Johann Sebastian Bach who?
Johann Sebastian Bach in town!

Knock–knock.
 Who's there?
John Q.
 John Q. who?
John Q. very much.

Knock–knock.
 Who's there?
Juan.
 Juan who?
Juan good turn
deserves another!

Knock–knock.
 Who's there?
Juana.
 Juana who?
Juana improve your
looks? Wear a mask.

Knock–knock.
　Who's there?
Juan.
　Juan who?
Juan two, buckle my shoe . . .

　Knock–knock.
　　Who's there?
　Grigor.
　　Grigor who?
　Grigor (three, four),
　shut the door . . .

　　Knock–knock.
　　　Who's there?
　　Physics.
　　　Physics who?
　　Physics (five, six),
　　pick up sticks.

　　　Knock–knock.
　　　　Who's there?
　　　Stefan Haight.
　　　　Stefan Haight who?
　　　Stefan Haight, lay them
　　　straight.

Knock–knock.
 Who's there?
Juarez.
 Juarez who?
Juarez you hiding,
you rascal you?

Knock–knock.
 Who's there?
Jubilee.
 Jubilee who?
Jubilee-ve in the
tooth fairy?

Knock–knock.
 Who's there?
Judah.
 Judah who?
Judah known by now if
you opened the door.

Knock–knock.
 Who's there?
Juicy Watt.
 Juicy Watt who?
Juicy Watt someone
wrote on your door?

Knock–knock.
   Who's there?
Juneau.
   Juneau who?
Juneau what time it is?

   Knock–knock.
      Who's there?
Nome.
      Nome who?
Nome, I don't.

      Knock–knock.
         Who's there?
Alaska.
         Alaska who?
Alaska someone else.

Knock–knock.
   Who's there?
Jupiter.
   Jupiter who?
Jupiter hurry or
you'll miss the
garbage truck.

   Knock–knock.
      Who's there?
Justin.
      Justin who?
Justin time for dinner.

Knock–knock.
   Who's there?
Justine.
   Justine who?
Justine old fashioned girl.

Knock–knock.
   Who's there?
Justis.
   Justis who?
Justis I thought.
Wrong door.

Knock-Knock!

Knock–knock.
 Who's there?
Kareem Cohen.
 Kareem Cohen who?
Ice Kareem Cohen!

Knock–knock.
 Who's there?
Keefe.
 Keefe who?
Keefe me one
more chance!

Knock–knock.
 Who's there?
Karen.
 Karen who?
Karen-teed to crack
you up!

Knock–knock.
   Who's there?
Keith.
   Keith who?
Keith me, you fool!

Knock–knock.
   Who's there?
Ken D.
   Ken D. who?
Ken D. Gram.

Knock–knock.
   Who's there?
Ken.
   Ken who?
Ken I come in?
It's freezing out here.

Knock–knock.
   Who's there?
Kenya.
   Kenya who?
Kenya hear me
knocking? I said
"Knock-Knock!"

Knock–knock.
   Who's there?
Kenya.
   Kenya who?
Kenya keep it
down in there?

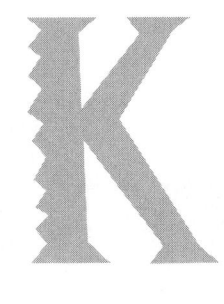

Knock–knock.
    Who's there?
Ketchup.
    Ketchup who?
Ketchup with me and
I'll tell you.

Knock–knock.
    Who's there?
Kevin.
    Kevin who?
"Thank Kevin for little girls . . ."

Knock–knock.
Who's there?
Kiefer.
Kiefer who?
Kiefer stiff upper lip.

Knock–knock.
Who's there?
Kimono.
Kimono who?
Kimono my house.

Knock–knock.
Who's there?
King Kong.
King Kong who?
"King Kong, the witch
is dead . . ."

Knock–knock.
Who's there?
Kip.
Kip who?
Kip talking. Maybe
you'll find something
to say.

K

Knock–knock.
Who's there?
Kipper.
Kipper who?
Kipper hands to
yourself.

Knock-knock.
    Who's there?
Klaus.
    Klaus who?
Klaus your mouth
and open the door!

Knock-knock.
    Who's there?
Koala.
    Koala who?
Koala-T jokes like these
are hard to find.

K

Knock-knock.
    Who's there?
Kojak.
    Kojak who?
Kojak up the car.
We've got a flat.

Knock-knock.
    Who's there?
Krakatoa.
    Krakatoa who?
Just Krakatoa trying to
kick this door down!

Knock-knock.
    Who's there?
Kris.
    Kris who?
Kris P. Critters!

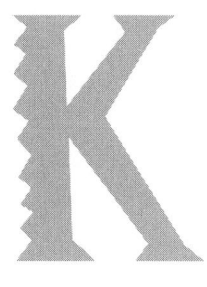

Knock–knock.
Who's there?
Kumquat.
Kumquat who?
Kumquat may, we'll always be buddies.

Knock–knock.
Who's there?
Kurt.
Kurt who?
Kurt that out!

Knock–knock.
Who's there?
Kurt and Conan.
Kurt and Cohan who?
Kurt and Conan (curtain coming) down on the last act.

Knock-Knock!

Knock–knock.
Who's there?
Lava.
Lava who?
"Lava, come back
to me . . ."

Knock–knock.
Who's there?
L.B.
L.B. who?
L.B. the judge of that!

Knock–knock.
Who's there?
Lee King.
Lee King who?
Lee King bucket.

Knock–knock.
Who's there?
Leah Penn.
Leah Penn who?
Leah Penn Lizards!

Knock–knock.
   Who's there?
Lemuel.
   Lemuel who?
Lemuel kicked me.
   Knock–knock.
      Who's there?
Thor.
      Thor who?
Thor all over.

Knock–knock.
   Who's there?
Lester.
      Lester who?
Lester the Red Hot
Mamas.

   Knock–knock.
      Who's there?
Lettuce.
      Lettuce who?
Lettuce in and we'll
tell you another
Knock-Knock joke.

Knock–knock.
   Who's there?
Leonie.
      Leonie who?
Leonie thing you
do fast is get tired.

   Knock–knock.
      Who's there?
Lettuce.
      Lettuce who?
Lettuce discuss this
like mature adults . . .

Knock–knock.
　Who's there?
Lima bean.
　Lima bean who?
"Lima bean (I've been)
working on the railroad . . ."

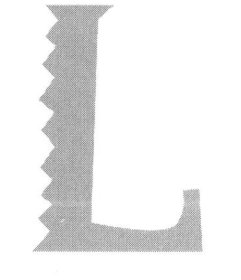

Knock–knock.
　Who's there?
Linda.
　Linda who?
Linda helping hand.
　Knock–knock.
　　Who's there?
Yukon.
　　Yukon who?
Yukon count on me.

　Knock–knock.
　　Who's there?
Lion.
　　Lion who?
Lion here on your doorstep
till you open the door.

Knock–knock.
　Who's there?
Lionel.
　Lionel who?
Lionel bite you if you
don't watch out.

Knock–knock.
　Who's there?
Lion.
　Lion who?
Lion down on the
job again?

Knock–knock.
　Who's there?
Lionel.
　Lionel who?
Lionel get you in
trouble!

L

Knock–knock.
　Who's there?
Lisa.
　Lisa who?
Lisa you can do
is let me in.

Knock–knock.
　Who's there?
Little old lady.
　Little old lady who?
I didn't know you could yodel.

Knock–knock.
Who's there?
Lucas Tell.
Lucas Tell who?
Lucas Tell-oh and
Bud Abbott.

Knock–knock.
Who's there?
Lotto.
Lotto who?
Lotto trouble coming
your way if you don't
open up.

Knock–knock.
Who's there?
Lucinda.
Lucinda who?
Lucinda chain and
let me inside.

Knock–knock.
 Who's there?
Lucretia.
 Lucretia who?
Lucretia (the creature)
from the Black Lagoon.

L

Knock–knock.
 Who's there?
Lucy.
 Lucy who?
Lucy Nupp!

Knock–knock.
 Who's there?
Lufthansa.
 Lufthansa who?
Lufthansa! This is a
stick-up!

Knock–knock.
　Who's there?
Luigi.
　Luigi who?
Luigi board.

Knock–knock.
　Who's there?
Luke.
　Luke who?
Luke before you leap.

Knock–knock.
　Who's there?
Luke.
　Luke who?
Luke through the
keyhole and see.

Knock–knock.
　Who's there?
Luke.
　Luke who?
Luke out below!

Knock–knock.
  Who's there?
Lyle.
  Lyle who?
Lyle be a monkey's
uncle!

Knock–knock.
  Who's there?
Lyndon.
  Lyndon who?
Lyndon ear and
I'll tell you.

Knock-Knock!

Scratch–scratch.
Who's there?
M-2.
M-2 who?
M-2 weak to knock.

Knock–knock.
Who's there?
Mabel.
Mabel who?
Mabel I'll tell you
and Mabel I won't!

Knock–knock.
Who's there?
Mack.
Mack who?
Mack up your mind!

Knock–knock.
Who's there?
Madge.
Madge who?
Madge N. that!

Knock–knock.
Who's there?
Madison.
Madison who?
You're Madison hatter!

Knock–knock.
    Who's there?
Ma Harrison.
    Ma Harrison who?
Ma Harrison (my hair is on) fire!

Knock–knock.
    Who's there?
Mamie.
    Mamie who?
The Devil Mamie
do it!

Knock–knock.
    Who's there?
Mandy.
    Mandy who?
Mandy lifeboats!
The ship is sinking!

Knock–knock.
    Who's there?
Mannheim.
    Mannheim who?
Mannheim tired!

M

Knock–knock.
　Who's there?
Manny Dunn.
　Manny Dunn who?
Manny Dunn grow on trees.

Knock–knock.
　Who's there?
Mansion.
　Mansion who?
Did I Mansion I have
more knock-knock jokes?

M

Knock–knock.
　Who's there?
Marmoset.
　Marmoset who?
Marmoset there'd be
days like this.

Knock–knock.
　Who's there?
Marsha.
　Marsha who?
Marsha Mallow!

Knock–knock.
Who's there?
Mary and Abbey.
Mary and Abbey who?
Mary Christmas and Abbey
New Year!

Knock–knock.
Who's there?
Maude.
Maude who?
Maude as well go home.

Knock–knock.
Who's there?
Mavis.
Mavis who?
Mavis be the last time
I knock at your door.

Knock–knock.
Who's there?
Math.
Math who?
Math (mashed)
Potatoes!

Knock–knock.
Who's there?
May Kay.
May Kay who?
May Kay while the
sun shines!

Knock–knock.
     Who's there?
Maynard.
     Maynard who?
Maynard come
around anymore
if you don't open up.

Knock–knock.
     Who's there?
Mayonnaise.
     Mayonnaise who?
"Mayonnaise have seen
the glory of the coming
of the Lord . . ."

Knock–knock.
     Who's there?
Mazda.
     Mazda who?
Mazda of the
Universe!

Knock–knock.
     Who's there?
Megan.
     Megan who?
Megan a phone call.

Knock–knock.
     Who's there?
Jessamyn.
     Jessamyn who?
Jessamyn-it please–
the lion is busy.

Knock–knock.
     Who's there?
Mustang.
     Mustang who?
Mustang up now–
I'm out of change.

M

Knock–knock.
    Who's there?
Megan, Elise and Chicken.
    Megan, Elise and Chicken who?
"He's Megan, Elise and Chicken it twice,
gonna find out who's naughty and nice . . ."

Knock–knock.
    Who's there?
Meteor.
    Meteor who?
Prepare to Meteor
(meet your) maker!

Knock–knock.
    Who's there?
Melissa.
    Melissa who?
Melissa to you and
I get in trouble.

Knock–knock.
Who's there?
Michael Rhoda.
Michael Rhoda who?
"Michael Rhoda boat ashore,
hallelujah . . ."

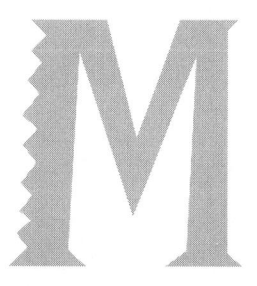

Knock–knock.
Who's there?
Midas.
Midas who?
Midas well try again—
knock-knock!

Knock–knock.
Who's there?
Mimi.
Mimi who?
Mimi at the pool. I'd like to
give you drowning lessons.

Knock–knock.
Who's there?
Meyer.
Meyer who?
Meyer in a nasty
mood!

M

Knock–knock.
Who's there?
Midas.
Midas who?
Midas well relax. I'm
not going any place.

Knock–knock.
Who's there?
Mike Rowe.
Mike Rowe who?
Mike Rowe wave oven.

Knock–knock.
   Who's there?
Mike Howe.
   Mike Howe who?
Mike Howe is sick.
   Knock–knock.
      Who's there?
Yvette.
      Yvette who?
Yvette fixed her up.

M

Knock–knock.
Who's there?
Mindy.
Mindy who?
Mindy mood for pizza.

Knock–knock.
Who's there?
Nova.
Nova who?
Nova good place for pizza?

Knock–knock.
Who's there?
Noah.
Noah who?
Noah don't.

Knock–knock.
Who's there?
Newton.
Newton who?
Newton Monday,
but I forgot.

Knock–knock.
　Who's there?
Minerva.
　Minerva who?
Minerva-s wreck from
all these questions.

Knock–knock.
　Who's there?
Minna.
　Minna who?
Minna wrong place
at the wrong time.

Knock–knock.
　Who's there?
Minneapolis.
　Minneapolis who?
Minneapolis each day
keep many doctors away.

Knock–knock.
　Who's there?
Mischief.
　Mischief who?
I guess I'd Mischief
(miss you if) you left . . .

Knock–knock.
　Who's there?
Miniature.
　Miniature who?
Miniature open your mouth,
you put your foot in it.

Knock–knock.
　Who's there?
Minnie.
　Minnie who?
No, not Minnie-who–
Minnehaha.

Knock–knock.
　Who's there?
Missouri.
　Missouri who?
Missouri (misery)
loves company!

Knock–knock.
Who's there?
Mohair.
Mohair who?
Any Mohair on your
head and you could
pass for a mop.

Knock–knock.
Who's there?
Morey and Les.
Morey and Les who?
The Morey I think of you,
the Les I think of you.

Knock–knock.
Who's there?
Morgan.
Morgan who?
Morgan just a pretty
face!

Knock–knock.
Who's there?
Mrs. S. Goode.
Mrs. S. Goode who?
A Mrs. S. Goode as a mile.

Knock–knock.
Who's there?
Mr. T.
Mr. T. who?
"Ah, sweet Mr. T. of life . . ."

Knock–knock.
Who's there?
Murray Lee.
Murray Lee who?
"Murray Lee we roll along . . ."

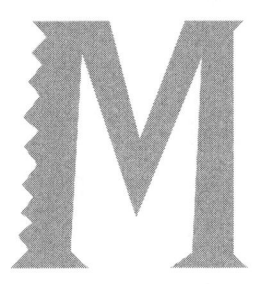

Knock–knock.
Who's there?
Musket.
Musket who?
Musket in! The Martians
are after me!

Knock–knock.
Who's there?
Mussolini.
Mussolini who?
Mussolini on your bell
for ten minutes.

Knock–knock.
Who's there?
Mustard Bean.
Mustard Bean who?
You Mustard Bean a big surprise
to your parents. They probably
expected a boy or girl.

Knock-Knock!

N

Knock–knock.
 Who's there?
Nanny.
 Nanny who?
Nanny my friends
like you either.

Knock–knock.
 Who's there?
Nanya.
 Nanya who?
Nanya Lip!

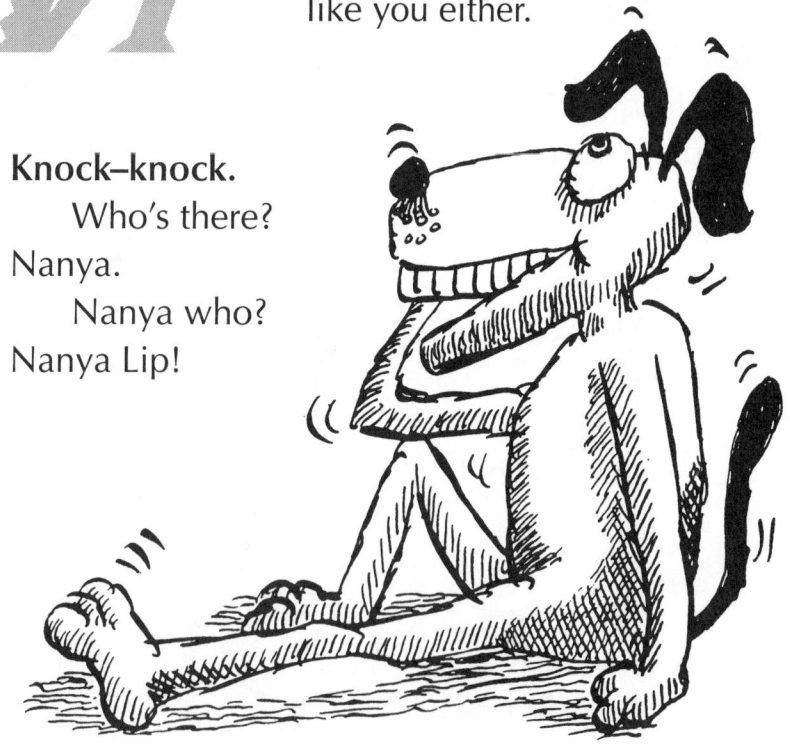

Knock–knock.
    Who's there?
N.E.
    N.E. who?
N.E. body you like, as
long as you let me in!

Knock–knock.
    Who's there?
Needle.
    Needle who?
Needle little attention.

    Knock–knock.
        Who's there?
    Needle.
        Needle who?
    Needle little help!

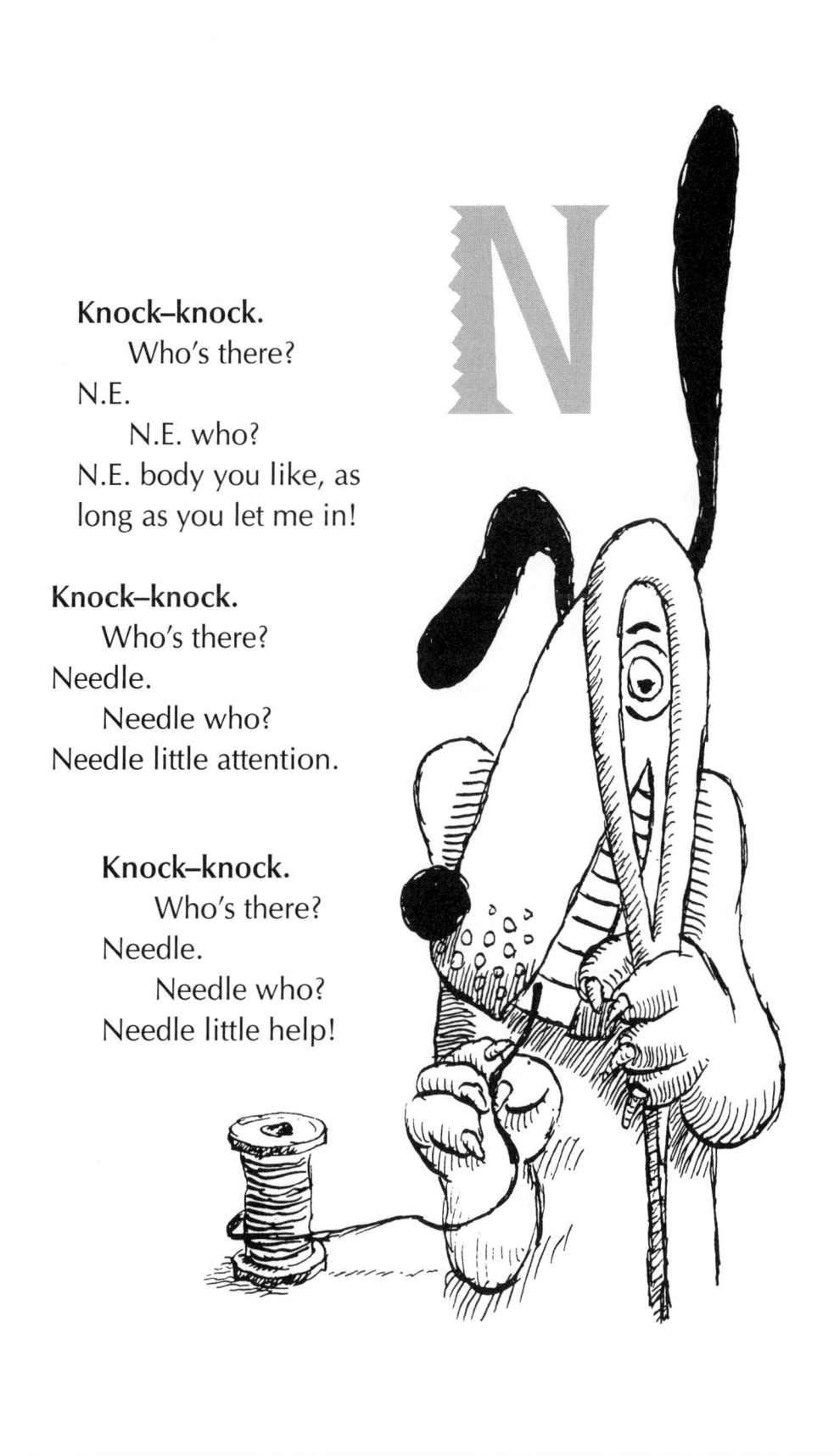

Knock–knock.
Who's there?
Nemo.
Nemo who?
Nemo time to think
of a joke!

Knock–knock.
Who's there?
Nefertiti.
Nefertiti who?
Nefertiti (never teeter)
totter with a 500-pound
gorilla!

Knock–knock.
Who's there?
Nevada.
Nevada who?
You Nevada had it so good!

Knock–knock.
Who's there?
Gouda.
Gouda who?
This is as Goudas it gets!

Knock–knock.
Who's there?
Osgood.
Osgood who?
Osgood S. Canby.

Knock–knock.
Who's there?
Nevil.
Nevil who?
Nevil mind!

Knock–knock.
Who's there?
Nevin.
Nevin who?
Nevin you mind—
just open up.

Knock–knock.
Who's there?
New Year.
New Year who?
New Year (knew you were)
going to say that!

Knock–knock.
Who's there?
Noah.
Noah who?
There's Noah-scape!

Knock–knock.
Who's there?
Nobel.
Nobel who?
Nobel, so I knocked.

Knock–knock.
Who's there?
Noodle.
Noodle who?
Never Noodle now
where you lived.

Knock–knock.
Who's there?
Nora Marx.
Nora Marx who?
Nora Marx (no remarks) from
the peanut gallery!

Knock–knock.
Who's there?
Avery.
Avery who?
Avery body's gettin' into
the act!

Knock–knock.
Who's there?
Norma Lee.
Norma Lee who?
Norma Lee I don't go around knocking on doors, but I have this wonderful set of encyclopedias . . .

Knock–knock.
Who's there?
Nutmeg.
Nutmeg who?
Nutmeg any difference what you say.

Knock–knock.
Who's there?
Nuisance.
Nuisance who?
What's nuisance yesterday?

Knock–knock.
Who's there?
Nurse.
Nurse who?
Nurse sense in talking to you.

Knock-Knock!

Knock–knock.
> Who's there?

Obi Wan.
> Obi Wan who?

Obi Wan-derful and take me to the movies!

Knock–knock.
> Who's there?

O'Casey.
> O'Casey who?

O'Casey if I care!

Knock–knock.
> Who's there?

Odaris.
> Odaris who?

Odaris a bee on your shoulder!

Knock–knock.
  Who's there?
Odd Thing.
  Odd Thing who?
Odd Thing (I'd sing) all
day if I knew a thong!

Knock–knock.
  Who's there?
Odysseus.
(Pronounced Oh-diss-us).
  Odysseus who?
Odysseus getting boring!

Knock–knock.
  Who's there?
Odysseus.
  Odysseus who?
Odysseus the last straw!

Knock–knock.
  Who's there?
Odyssey.
  Odyssey who?
Odyssey (hard to see)
how you made it past
the first grade!

Knock–knock.
  Who's there?
Offer.
  Offer who?
Offer got (I forgot)!

Knock–knock.
  Who's there?
Office.
  Office who?
He's Office rocker.

Knock–knock.
Who's there?
Ogre.
Ogre who?
Ogre take a flying leap!

Knock–knock.
Who's there?
Ohio.
Ohio who?
Ohio feeling?

Knock–knock.
Who's there?
Kentucky.
Kentucky who?
Kentucky (can't talk) too
well, have a soar throat.

Knock–knock.
Who's there?
Nevada.
Nevada who?
Nevada saw you look worse.
You should be in bed.

Knock–knock.
Who's there?
Ohio.
Ohio who?
Ohio Silver!

Knock–knock.
Who's there?
Ohio.
Ohio who?
Ohio feeling?

Knock–knock.
Who's there?
Oink.
Oink who?
Oink L. Sam!

Knock–knock.
   Who's there?
O'Keefe.
   O'Keefe who?
"O'Keefe me a home
where the buffalo
roam . . ."

Knock–knock.
   Who's there?
Olga.
   Olga who?
Olga home if you
don't treat me better.

Knock–knock.
   Who's there?
Olivia.
   Olivia who?
Olivia (I live here)
but I forgot my key.

Knock–knock.
> Who's there?

Olivia.
> Olivia who?

Olivia lone if that's what you want!

Knock–knock.
> Who's there?

Olivia.
> Olivia who?

Olivia me alone!

Knock–knock.
> Who's there?

Ollie-Lou.
> Ollie-Lou who?

Ollie-Lou ya! You finally opened the door!

Knock–knock.
> Who's there?

Ollie or Rex.
> Ollie or Rex who?

Don't put Ollie or Rex in one basket.

Knock–knock.
Who's there?
Ollie.
Ollie who?
Ollie time you say that,
I wish you'd cut it out.

Knock–knock.
Who's there?
Omaha.
Omaha who?
Omaha goodness! My hand
is caught in the door!

Knock–knock.
Who's there?
Omar.
Omar who?
Omar goodness gracious!
Wrong door!

Knock–knock.
Who's there?
Omega.
Omega who?
Omega best man win!

Knock–knock.
Who's there?
Omega.
Omega who?
Omega up your mind.

Knock–knock.
  Who's there?
Ooze.
  Ooze who?
Ooze in charge
around here?

Knock–knock.
  Who's there?
Opossum.
  Opossum who?
Opossum by and
thought I'd say hello.

Knock–knock.
  Who's there?
Orangutan.
  Orangutan who?
Orangutan times but
you didn't answer.

Knock–knock.
  Who's there?
Orbach.
  Orbach who?
Front Orbach–
you look awful.

Knock–knock.
Who's there?
Osaka.
Osaka who?
Osaka to me!
Knock–knock.
Who's there?
Oxford.
Oxford who?
You Oxford it! (*Pow!*)

Knock–knock.
Who's there?
Oscar and Greta.
Oscar and Greta who?
Oscar foolish question and
Greta a foolish answer.

Knock–knock.
Who's there?
O'Shea.
O'Shea who?
O'Shea it isn't so.

Knock–knock.
Who's there?
Oslo.
Oslo who?
Oslo on cash.
How about a little loan?

Knock–knock.
  Who's there?
Otto B.
  Otto B. who?
Otto B. a law against people like you.

Knock–knock.
  Who's there?
Otto.
  Otto who?
Your bell is Otto order.

Knock–knock.
  Who's there?
Owen Williams.
  Owen Williams who?
Owen Williams
(oh, when will you)
open this door?

Knock–knock.
  Who's there?
Oz.
  Oz who?
Oz out here freezing.

Knock-Knock!

Knock–knock.
　　Who's there?
Panda.
　　Panda who?
Panda monium!

Knock–knock.
　　Who's there?
Passion.
　　Passion who?
Passion by and thought
I'd say hello.

Knock–knock.
　　Who's there?
Pasteur.
　　Pasteur who?
It's Pasteur (past your)
bedtime!

Knock–knock.
Who's there?
Pasta.
Pasta who?
Pasta pizza under the door–I'm starved!

Knock–knock.
Who's there?
Azenauer.
Azenauer who?
Azenauer (has an hour) gone by
since you put the pizza in the oven?

Knock–knock.
Who's there?
Patton.
Patton who?
Patton leather shoes!

Knock–knock.
Who's there?
Paul.
Paul who?
Paul-tergeist!

Knock–knock.
Who's there?
Peapod.
Peapod who?
I don't want to hear a
Peapod (peep out of) you!

Knock–knock.
Who's there?
Pekingese.
Pekingese who?
Pekingese through the peephole and see.

Knock–knock.
Who's there?
Phineas.
Phineas who?
Phineas thing happened on the way over here . . .

Knock–knock.
Who's there?
Percy.
Percy who?
Percy-veere (persevere)!

Knock–knock.
Who's there?
Phyllis.
Phyllis who?
Phyllis in on the details!

Knock–knock.
Who's there?
Pinafore.
Pinafore who?
Pinafore for your thoughts . . .

Knock–knock.
Who's there?
Pitcher.
Pitcher who?
Pitcher money where
your mouth is!

Knock–knock.
Who's there?
Pizza.
Pizza who?
Pizza nice guy when
you get to know him.

Knock–knock.
Who's there?
Plato.
Plato who?
Plato spaghetti and meatballs, please.

Knock–knock.
Who's there?
Police.
Police who?
Police open the door!

Knock–knock.
Who's there?
Police.
Police who?
Police B. Careful!

Knock–knock.
   Who's there?
Polly N.
   Polly N. who?
Polly N. saturated.

Knock–knock.
   Who's there?
Possum.
   Possum who?
Possum peace pipe.

Knock–knock.
   Who's there?
Pumpkin.
   Pumpkin who?
A thing that goes
pumpkin (bump in)
the night.

Knock–knock.
   Who's there?
Porsche.
   Porsche who?
Porsche me in the
right direction!

Knock–knock.
   Who's there?
Preston.
   Preston who?
Preston the doorbell,
but it won't ring.

Knock–knock.
   Who's there?
Pudding.
   Pudding who?
Pudding my best
foot forward!

P

Knock–knock.
 Who's there?
Punch.
 Punch who?
Not me–
I just got here!

Knock–knock.
 Who's there?
Pyrite.
 Pyrite who?
Pyrite in your face—Pow!

Knock-Knock!

Knock–knock.
    Who's there?
Quacker.
    Quacker who?
Quacker 'nother bad joke
and I'm leaving.

      Knock–knock.
         Who's there?
      Quebec.
         Quebec who?
      Quebec to the end
      of the line.

Knock–knock.
    Who's there?
Quibble.
    Quibble who?
Quibble and Bits.

Knock–knock.
    Who's there?
Quiet Tina.
    Quiet Tina who?
Quiet Tina courtroom–
monkey wants to speak.

Knock–knock.
    Who's there?
Quigley.
    Quigley who?
Open the door Quigley,
I must get in!

Knock-Knock!

Knock–knock.
   Who's there?
Radio.
   Radio who?
Radio not, here
I come!

Knock–knock.
   Who's there?
Raisin.
   Raisin who?
Raisin Cane!

Knock–knock.
   Who's there?
Rajah.
   Rajah who?
Rajah Rabbit!

Knock–knock.
Who's there?
Ralph.
Ralph who?
Ralph! Ralph! I'm a puppy dog!

Knock–knock.
Who's there?
Rambo.
Rambo who?
"Somewhere, over the Rambo . . ."

Knock–knock.
Who's there?
Ramona.
Ramona who?
Ramona going to ask you once more . . .

Knock–knock.
Who's there?
Randall.
Randall who?
Randall the way from the bus.

R

Knock–knock.
   Who's there?
Raoul (pronounced Rah-*ool*).
   Raoul who?
"Raoul out the barrel . . ."

Knock–knock.
   Who's there?
A Raven.
   A Raven who?
A Raven Maniac.

Knock–knock.
   Who's there?
Ray and Greta.
   Ray and Greta who?
You'll Ray Greta asking
me that!

Knock–knock.
   Who's there?
Rector.
   Rector who?
Rector car. Can I
use your phone?

Knock–knock.
> Who's there?
Renata.
> Renata who?
Renata (run out of) steam?

Knock–knock.
> Who's there?
Reverend.
> Reverend who?
For Reverend ever I've
been standing out here . . .

Knock–knock.
> Who's there?
Rhett.
> Rhett who?
Rhett-urn of the Jedi.

Knock–knock.
> Who's there?
Rhonda.
> Rhonda who?
Rhonda arrest!

Knock–knock.
> Who's there?
Rick.
> Rick who?
Rick Shaw, hop in
for a ride!

Knock–knock.
Who's there?
Ringo.
Ringo who?
Ringo round the collar.

Knock–knock.
Who's there?
Ripon.
Ripon who?
Ripon up your welcome mat.

Knock–knock.
Who's there?
Rise and Follow.
Rise and Follow who?
Rise and Follow (rise and fall of) the Roman Empire.

Knock–knock.
Who's there?
Rita.
Rita who?
Rita my lips!

Knock–knock.
　Who's there?
Robert de Niro.
　Robert de Niro who?
Robert de Niro, but he's
not here yet.

Knock–knock.
　Who's there?
Robert Redford.
　Robert Redford who?
Robert Redford the part in
the play.

Knock–knock.
　Who's there?
Rollin.
　Rollin who?
"As we come rollin'
rollin' home . . ."

Knock–knock.
　Who's there?
Roman.
　Roman who?
Roman around with
nothing to do.

Knock–knock.
　Who's there?
Romanoff.
　Romanoff who?
There ain't Romanoff for the
both of us in this town!

Knock–knock.
　Who's there?
Ronan.
　Ronan who?
Ronan amuck!

Knock–knock.
Who's there?
Ron.
Ron who?
Ron for your life!

Knock–knock.
Who's there?
Rover.
Rover who?
It's all Rover between us.

Knock–knock.
Who's there?
Roxanne.
Roxanne who?
Roxanne your head
or something?

Knock–knock.
Who's there?
Rona.
Rona who?
Rona the mill.

Knock–knock.
Who's there?
Roy.
Roy who?
Roy L. Flush!

Knock-knock.
   Who's there?
Rubber Duck.
   Rubber Duck who?
"Rubber Duck dub–
three men in a tub . . ."

Knock–knock.
   Who's there?
Rumania.
   Rumania who?
Can't Rumania out here
much longer.

Knock–knock.
   Who's there?
Rufus.
   Rufus who?
Rufus leaking and
I'm getting wet.

Knock–knock.
   Who's there?
Russ.
   Russ who?
Russ Crispies!

Knock-Knock!

Knock–knock.
Who's there?
Sadie.
Sadie who?
Sadie Pledge of
Allegiance.

Knock–knock.
Who's there?
Safari.
Safari who?
Safari so good.

Knock–knock.
Who's there?
Safaris.
Safaris who?
Safaris I can see,
it's me!

Knock–knock.
Who's there?
Salem.
Salem who?
Salem away for good–never
have to see you again.

Knock–knock.
Who's there?
Sam and Janet.
Sam and Janet who?
"Sam and Janet evening,
you will meet a stranger . . ."

Knock–knock.
Who's there?
Salada.
Salada who?
Salada bad Knock-Knock
jokes around.

Knock–knock.
Who's there?
Sam.
Sam who?
Sam old story.
Ho-hum.

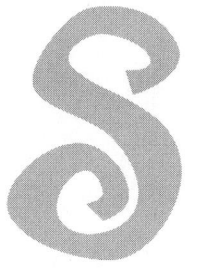

Knock–knock.
Who's there?
Samovar.
Samovar who?
Samovar time you
can be a real pest.

Knock–knock.
Who's there?
Sancho.
Sancho who?
Sancho a letter, but
you never answered.

Knock–knock.
Who's there?
Sanctuary.
Sanctuary who?
Sanctuary much.

Knock–knock.
Who's there?
Santa Ana.
Santa Ana who?
Santa Ana coming
to your house because
you've been bad.

Knock–knock.
Who's there?
Santa.
Santa who?
Santa Mental Fool!

Knock–knock.
Who's there?
Santucci.
Santucci who?
Santucci my sunburn!

Knock–knock.
  Who's there?
Satin.
  Satin who?
Who Satin my chair?

Knock–knock.
Who's there?
Satellite.
Satellite who?
Satellite in the window—
one if by land,
two if by sea.

Knock–knock.
 Who's there?
Sarah.
 Sarah who?
Sarah doctor in
the house?

Knock–knock.
 Who's there?
Sarong and Sari.
 Sarong and Sari who?
Sarong house. Sari.

Knock–knock.
 Who's there?
Sasha.
 Sasha who?
Sasha dummy!

Knock–knock.
 Who's there?
Saul and Terry.
 Saul and Terry who?
Saul and Terry confinement!

Knock–knock.
 Who's there?
Saul Upp.
 Saul Upp who?
Saul Upp to you!

Knock–knock.
　Who's there?
Schick.
　Schick who?
I'm Schick as a dog.

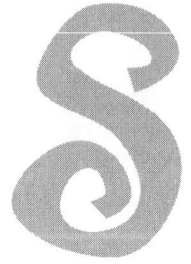

　Knock–knock.
　　Who's there?
Esau.
　　Esau who?
Esau throat is killing me.

　　Knock–knock.
　　　Who's there?
Consuelo.
　　　Consuelo who?
Consuelo a thing.

　　　Knock–knock.
　　　　Who's there?
Gargoyle.
　　　　Gargoyle who?
Gargoyle with salt water
and you'll feel better.

　　　　Knock–knock.
　　　　　Who's there?
Hatch.
　　　　　Hatch who?
I didn't know you
were sick, too.

Knock–knock.
Who's there?
Schatzi.
Schatzi who?
Schatzi way the
ball bounces.

Knock–knock.
Who's there?
Schenectady.
Schenectady who?
Schenectady (the neck
of the) shirt is too tight.

Knock–knock.
Who's there?
Scissor.
Scissor who?
Scissor and Cleopatra.

Knock–knock.
Who's there?
Scoot.
Scoot who?
Scoot to be here!

Knock–knock.
Who's there?
Scold.
Scold who?
Scold outside.

Knock–knock.
Who's there?
Sea Bass.
Sea Bass who?
Sea Bass-tian the crab.

Knock–knock.
Who's there?
Scott.
Scott who?
Scott to be me!

Knock–knock.
   Who's there?
Seashell.
   Seashell who?
"Seashell have music
wherever she goes . . ."

Knock–knock.
   Who's there?
Seiko.
   Seiko who?
"Seiko and ye shall
find . . ."

Knock–knock.
   Who's there?
Seminole.
   Seminole who?
"Seminole cowhand–
from the Rio Grande . . ."

Knock–knock.
Who's there?
Senior.
Senior who?
Senior through the peephole, so I know you're in there.

Knock–knock.
Who's there?
Seth.
Seth who?
Seth me, that's who.

Knock–knock.
Who's there?
Seymour.
Seymour who?
Seymour if you'd get the door open.

Knock–knock.
Who's there?
Shelley.
Shelley who?
Shelley try again?
Knock–knock.
Who's there?
Dozen.
Dozen who?
Dozen matter to me!

Knock–knock.
  Who's there?
Sheila.
  Sheila who?
"Sheila be coming
round the mountain
when she comes . . ."

Knock–knock.
  Who's there?
Sharon.
  Sharon who?
Sharon share alike.

Knock–knock.
  Who's there?
Shafter.
  Shafter who?
Shafter make a
phone call!

Knock–knock.
  Who's there?
Shirley M.
  Shirley M. who?
Shirley M. glad to say
goodbye to you.

Knock–knock.
Who's there?
Shoe buckle.
Shoe buckle who?
Shoe buckle up your seat belt?

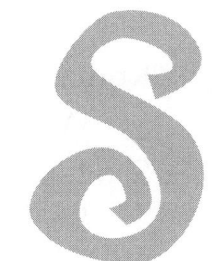

Knock–knock.
Who's there?
Shoes.
Shoes who?
Shoes me, I must
have knocked on
the wrong door.

Knock–knock.
Who's there?
Shopper Dan.
Shopper Dan who?
You're Shopper Dan
(sharper than) I thought!

Knock–knock.
Who's there?
Siam.
Siam who?
Siam your old pal.

Knock–knock.
Who's there?
Sid.
Sid who?
"Sid-down, you're
rocking the boat . . ."

Knock–knock.
Who's there?
Siamese.
Siamese who?
Siamese-y to please.

Knock–knock.
    Who's there?
Sigrid.
    Sigrid who?
Sigrid Service—
open up!

Knock–knock.
    Who's there?
Simon.
    Simon who?
"Simon the mood
for love . . ."

Knock–knock.
    Who's there?
Simms.
    Simms who?
Simms like I'm always
knocking on doors.

Knock–knock.
    Who's there?
Sinatra.
    Sinatra who?
Sinatra the cough
that carries you off,
it's the coffin they
carry you off in.

Knock–knock.
    Who's there?
Sincerely.
    Sincerely who?
Sincerely this morning
I've been listening to
Knock-Knock jokes.

Knock–knock.
    Who's there?
Sis.
    Sis who?
Sis any way to
treat a friend?

Knock–knock.
Who's there?
Sloan.
Sloan who?
Sloan (slow and)
steady wins the race!

Knock–knock.
Who's there?
Sly Dover.
Sly Dover who?
Sly Dover, I'm breaking
down the door!

Knock–knock.
Who's there?
Snow.
Snow who?
Snow use talking
to you.

Knock–knock.
Who's there?
Sodium.
Sodium who?
Sodium (so do you)
mind if I come in?

Knock–knock.
Who's there?
Sony.
Sony who?
Sony your old pal . . .
Knock–knock.
Who's there?
Trotter.
Trotter who?
Trotter remember me.

Knock–knock.
    Who's there?
Sonny N.
    Sonny N. who?
Sonny N. clear today–
rain tomorrow!

Knock–knock.
    Who's there?
Sony and Toshiba.
    Sony and Toshiba who?
Sony me, waiting Toshiba.

Knock–knock.
    Who's there?
Spetzel.
    Spetzel who?
Spetzel delivery!

Knock–knock.
    Who's there?
Spook.
    Spook who?
I spook too soon!

Knock–knock.
    Who's there?
Stan.
    Stan who?
Stan back–I'm knocking
the door down.

Knock–knock.
    Who's there?
Stan and Bea.
    Stan and Bea who?
Stan Dupp and Bea
Counted!

Knock–knock.
    Who's there?
Stella.
    Stella who?
Stella no answer
at the door.

Knock–knock.
    Who's there?
Stencil.
    Stencil who?
Stencil–there's a
bee on your nose.

Knock–knock.
    Who's there?
Sue.
    Sue who?
Sue-prise–it's me!

Knock–knock.
Who's there?
Sumatra.
Sumatra who?
What's Sumatra with you?

Knock–knock.
Who's there?
Sven.
Sven who?
Sven are you going
to open the door?

Knock–knock.
Who's there?
Swatter.
Swatter who?
Swatter you complaining
about now?

Knock–knock.
Who's there?
Surreal.
Surreal who?
Surreal pleasure
to be here!

Knock–knock.
Who's there?
Swann.
Swann who?
"Just Swann of those
things . . ."

Knock–knock.
Who's there?
Sybil.
Sybil who?
Sybil War!

Knock–knock.
Who's there?
Sycamore.
Sycamore who?
Sycamore Knock-Knock jokes.

Knock-Knock!

Knock–knock.
 Who's there?
Tamara.
 Tamara who?
Tamara Boom-dee-ay!

Knock–knock.
 Who's there?
Tasmania.
 Tasmania who?
Tasmania slip between
the cup and the lip.

Knock–knock.
 Who's there?
Taurus.
 Taurus who?
Taurus closed on
my foot. Ouch!

T

Knock–knock.
Who's there?
Tennessee.
Tennessee who?
Tennessee you tonight?

Knock–knock.
Who's there?
Tamara.
Tamara who?
Tamara would be better.

Knock–knock.
Who's there?
Tennessee.
Tennessee who?
Is that a Tennessee
(tan I see), or haven't
you bathed lately?

Knock–knock.
Who's there?
Terrify.
Terrify who?
Terrify tissue?

Knock–knock.
Who's there?
Tess Slater.
Tess Slater who?
Tess Slater than you think!

210

Knock–knock.
    Who's there?
Thaddeus.
    Thaddeus who?
Thaddeus the silliest
thing I ever heard.

Knock–knock.
    Who's there?
Thayer.
    Thayer who?
Thayer thorry and I won't
throw this pie in your face.

Knock–knock.
    Who's there?
Thea.
    Thea who?
Thea later, alligator.

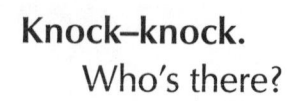

Knock–knock.
    Who's there?
Thelonius.
    Thelonius who?
Thelonius kid in town.

Knock–knock.
    Who's there?
The Genius.
    The Genius who?
The Genius (the genie is)
out of the bottle.

Knock–knock.
    Who's there?
The Ghost.
    The Ghost who?
The Ghost is clear—
let's go!

Knock–knock.
    Who's there?
Theodore.
    Theodore who?
Theodore is closed,
open up!

Knock–knock.
    Who's there?
Theonie.
    Theonie who?
Theonie trouble with
your face is that it shows.

Knock–knock.
    Who's there?
Theophilus.
    Theophilus who?
Theophilus person I ever
met is you.

Knock–knock.
Who's there?
Thistle.
Thistle who?
Thistle be the last time
I knock on your door.

Knock–knock.
Who's there?
Theresa.
Theresa who?
Theresa fly in my soup.

Knock–knock.
Who's there?
Threadbare.
Threadbare who?
Threadbare-n (the Red Baron)
and Snoopy the Flying Ace.

Knock–knock.
Who's there?
Thud.
Thud who?
Thud you'd never ask!

Knock–knock.
Who's there?
Thurston.
Thurston who?
Thurston for some water.

Knock–knock.
Who's there?
Tibet.
Tibet who?
Early Tibet and
early to rise . . .

Knock–knock.
Who's there?
Tick.
Tick who?
Tick 'em up!

Knock–knock.
Who's there?
Tijuana.
Tijuana who?
Tijuana try for two
out of three?

Knock–knock.
Who's there?
Tinker Bell.
Tinker Bell who?
Tinker Bell is out of
order.

Knock–knock.
Who's there?
Titus.
Titus who?
Titus string around your
finger so you won't forget
to open the door.

T

Knock–knock.
    Who's there?
Toad.
    Toad who?
Toad you before,
but you forgot.

Knock–knock.
Who's there?
Tobias.
Tobias who?
Are you going Tobias more
Knock-Knock books.

Knock–knock.
Who's there?
Toledo.
Toledo who?
It's easy Toledo horse to water,
but you can't make him drink.

Knock–knock.
Who's there?
Tom Hills.
Tom Hills who?
Tom Hills (time heals)
all wounds!

Knock–knock.
Who's there?
Tommy.
Tommy who?
I have a Tommy Ache!

Knock–knock.
Who's there?
Toodle-oo.
Toodle-oo who?
"Skip Toodle-oo,
my darling . . ."

Knock–knock.
Who's there?
Toodle.
Toodle who?
Bye-bye.

Knock–knock.
Who's there?
Toothache.
Toothache who?
Toothache the high road
and I'll take the low road.

Knock–knock.
Who's there?
Top Hat.
Top Hat who?
Top Hat (stop that–
you're bothering me!

Knock–knock.
Who's there?
Topeka.
Topeka who?
Don't open the door.
I like Topeka through
keyholes.

Knock–knock.
Who's there?
Topol.
Topol who?
"On Topol Old
Smokey . . ."

Knock–knock.
Who's there?
Toreador.
Toreador who?
Toreador down–now can I come in?

Knock–knock.
Who's there?
Toronto.
Toronto who?
Have Toronto the store.
Can I get you anything?

Knock–knock.
Who's there?
Canada.
Canada who?
Canada best dog food.

Knock–knock.
Who's there?
Toulouse.
Toulouse who?
Want Toulouse ten ugly
pounds? Cut off your head.

Knock–knock.
　Who's there?
Trigger.
　Trigger who?
Trigger treat!

Knock–knock.
　Who's there?
Troy.
　Troy who?
Troy as I may,
I can't reach the bell.

Knock–knock.
　Who's there?
Troy.
　Troy who?
Troy again!
　Knock–knock.
　　Who's there?
Wes D.
　　Wes D. who?
Wes D. point?

Knock–knock.
　Who's there?
Trudy.
　Trudy who?
Can I come Trudy window?
The door is stuck.

Knock–knock.
Who's there?
Truman E.
Truman E. who?
Truman E. cooks spoil
the broth!

Knock–knock.
Who's there?
Turner.
Turner who?
Turner round. You look
better from the back.

Knock–knock.
Who's there?
Two badgers.
Two badgers who?
Two badgers got a chip
on your shoulder.

Knock-Knock!

U

Knock–knock.
Who's there?
U-Boat.
U-Boat who?
U-Boat me a present?

Knock–knock.
Who's there?
Udall.
Udall who?
Udall know if you
opened the door.

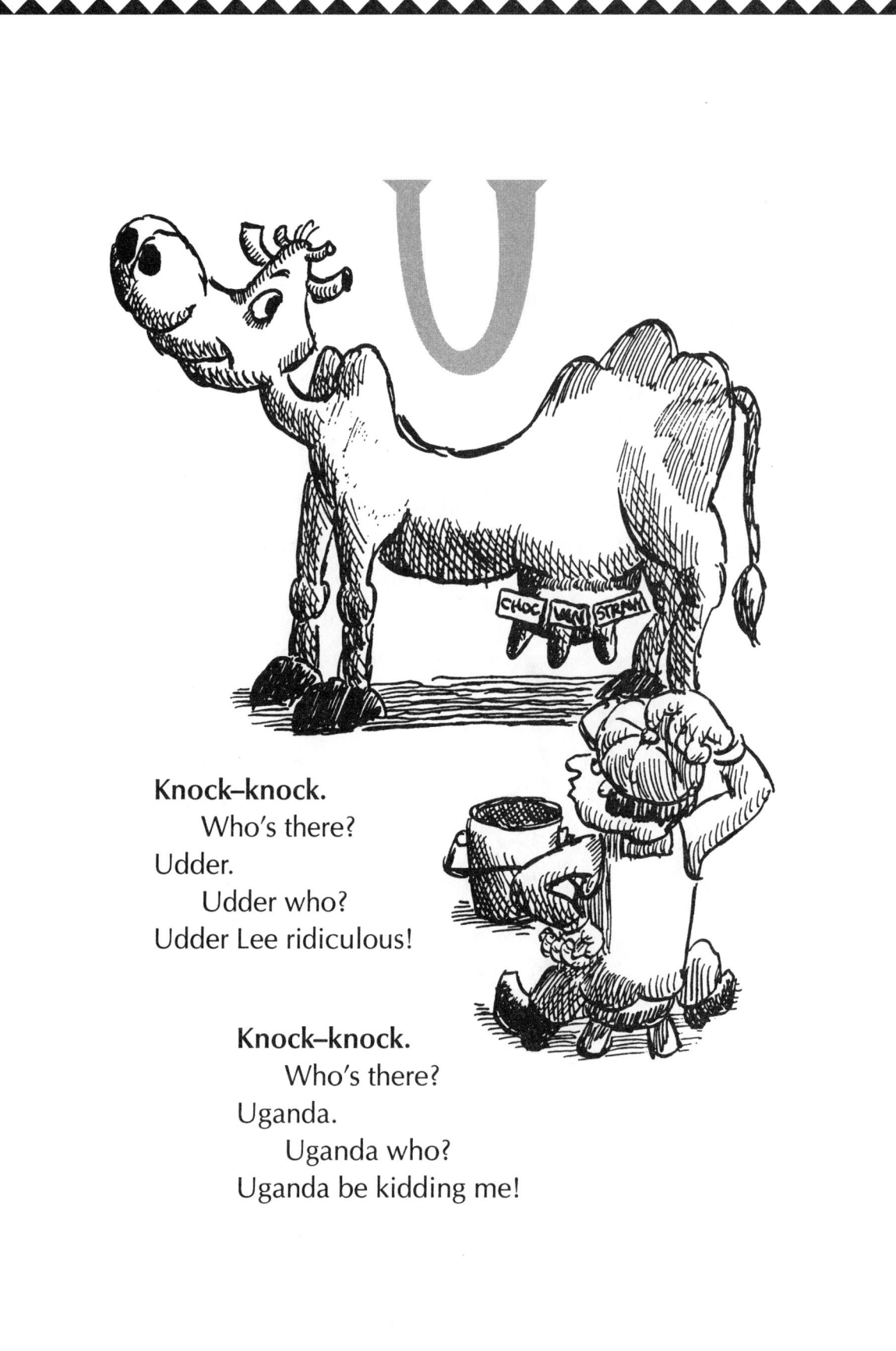

Knock–knock.
    Who's there?
Udder.
    Udder who?
Udder Lee ridiculous!

Knock–knock.
    Who's there?
Uganda.
    Uganda who?
Uganda be kidding me!

Knock–knock.
　　Who's there?
Uganda.
　　Uganda who?
Uganda get away
with this.

Knock–knock.
　　Who's there?
Uganda.
　　Uganda who?
Uganda never guess.

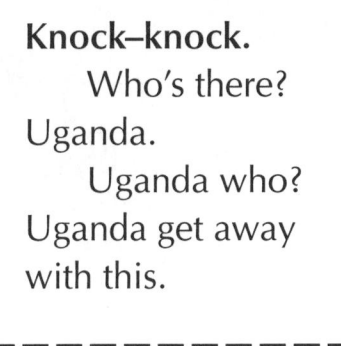

Knock–knock.
　　Who's there?
Unaware.
　　Unaware who?
Your unaware has a hole in it!

Knock–knock.
　　Who's there?
Tom Sawyer.
　　Tom Sawyer who?
Tom Sawyer underwear.

Knock–knock.
　　Who's there?
Arkansas.
　　Arkansas who?
Arkansas it, too!

Knock–knock.
　　Who's there?
Esau.
　　Esau who?
Esau it too.

Knock–knock.
Who's there?
Unique.
Unique who?
Why do Unique
(you sneak)
around on tiptoe?

Knock–knock.
Who's there?
Unicorn.
Unicorn who?
Unicorn-iest guy I ever met.

U

Knock–knock.
Who's there?
Unity.
Unity who?
Unity sweater for me?

Knock–knock.
Who's there?
Upton.
Upton who?
Upton no good,
as usual.

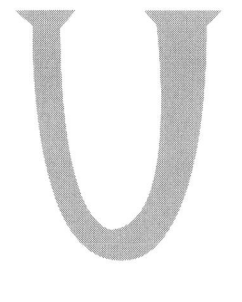

Knock–knock.
　Who's there?
Ural.
　Ural who?
Ural washed up, kid!

Knock–knock.
　Who's there?
Uriah.
　Uriah who?
Keep Uriah on the ball.

Knock–knock.
　Who's there?
Uruguay.
　Uruguay who?
You go Uruguay and
I'll go mine.

Knock–knock.
　Who's there?
Usher.
　Usher who?
Usher wish you would
let me in.

Knock–knock.
　Who's there?
Utah-Nevada.
　Utah-Nevada who?
Utah-Nevada guessed if
I didn't tell you.

Knock–knock.
Who's there?
Uta May.
Uta May who?
Going Uta May mind!

Knock–knock.
Who's there?
Uta.
Uta who?
Uta sight, uta mind.

Knock–knock.
Who's there?
Utica.
Utica who?
Utica high road and I'll
take the low road.

Knock-Knock!

V

Knock–knock.
Who's there?
Vacancy.
Vacancy who?
Vacancy (we can see)
right in your window!

Knock–knock.
Who's there?
Valley.
Valley who?
Valley intellesting!

Knock–knock.
Who's there?
Vanna White.
Vanna White who?
Vanna White (want to
write) your name on this
dotted line?

Knock–knock.
Who's there?
Vasilli.
Vasilli who?
Vasilli (what a silly)
person you are!

Knock–knock.
   Who's there?
Van Gogh.
   Van Gogh who?
Ready–set–Van Gogh!

Knock–knock.
   Who's there?
Vaudeville.
   Vaudeville who?
Vaudeville (what will)
you be doing tonight?

Knock–knock.
   Who's there?
Vaughan.
   Vaughan who?
Vaughan to come
over tomorrow?

Knock–knock.
   Who's there?
Vassar girl.
   Vassar girl who?
Vassar girl like you doing
in a place like this?

Knock–knock.
   Who's there?
Vaughan.
   Vaughan who?
"Vaughan day my
prince will come . . ."

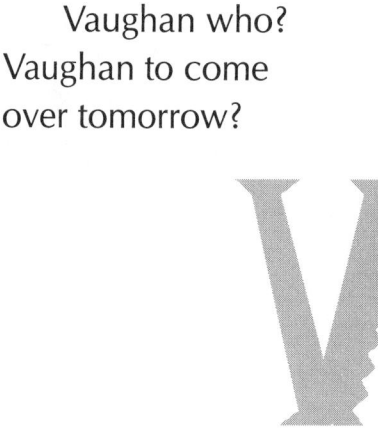

Knock–knock.
　Who's there?
Veal chop.
　Veal chop who?
Veal chop for a used car.

Knock–knock.
　Who's there?
Vehicle.
　Vehicle who?
Don't call us–
Vehicle (we will call) you!

Knock–knock
　Who's there?
Venice.
　Venice who?
Venice these Knock-Knock
jokes going to stop?

Knock–knock.
　Who's there?
Ventriloquist.
　Ventriloquist who?
Ventriloquist-mas tree
get decorated?

Knock–knock.
　Who's there?
Venus.
　Venus who?
Venus see you,
I feel sick.

Knock–knock.
　Who's there?
Veronica.
　Veronica who?
Veronica (we're on a c-)razy diet.

Knock–knock.
    Who's there?
Vera.
    Vera who?
"Vera all the flowers
gone . . ."

Knock–knock.
    Who's there?
Vicious.
    Vicious who?
Best Vicious!

Knock–knock.
    Who's there?
Vi.
    Vi who?
Vi not?!

Knock–knock.
    Who's there?
Vienna.
    Vienna who?
Zis is Vienna the book.

Knock–knock.
    Who's there?
Vile.
    Vile who?
Vile the cat's away,
the mice vill play!

V

Knock–knock.
    Who's there?
Vilma.
    Vilma who?
Vilma frog turn
into a prince?

Knock–knock.
    Who's there?
Vilma.
    Vilma who?
Vilma dreams come true?

Knock–knock.
Who's there?
Viola.
Viola who?
Viola sudden you
don't know me?

Knock–knock.
Who's there?
Violet.
Violet who?
Violet the cat out
of the bag?

Knock–knock.
Who's there?
Virtue.
Virtue who?
Virtue get those big,
brown eyes?

Knock–knock.
Who's there?
Virus.
Virus who?
Virus you always
singing stupid songs?

Knock–knock.
Who's there?
Viscount.
(Pronounced V-eye-count)
Viscount who?
Viscount you behave?

Knock–knock.
Who's there?
Voodoo.
Voodoo who?
Voodoo you think you
are, the Wolf Man?

Knock-Knock!

Knock–knock.
   Who's there?
Waco (pronounced Wake-o)
and El Paso.
   Waco and El Paso who?
If I can stay Waco for the test,
I think El Paso.

Knock–knock.
   Who's there?
Wallaby.
   Wallaby who?
Wallaby in trouble
if I keep knocking
on the door?

Knock–knock.
   Who's there?
Walter D.
   Walter D. who?
Walter D. Lawn.

Knock–knock.
    Who's there?
Waddle.
    Waddle who?
Waddle I need to
do to get you to use
your brain?

Knock–knock.
    Who's there?
Waiter.
    Waiter who?
Waiter-ound and
you'll see!

Knock–knock.
    Who's there?
Wadsworth.
    Wadsworth who?
Wadsworth it to you if
I go away?

Knock–knock.
    Who's there?
Wanamaker.
    Wanamaker who?
Wanamaker mud pie?

Knock–knock.
    Who's there?
Wanda.
    Wanda who?
Wanda come out
and play?

Knock–knock.
    Who's there?
Wanda.
    Wanda who?
Wanda these days—Pow!

W

Knock–knock.
Who's there?
Warden.
Warden who?
Warden the world
are you up to?

Knock–knock.
Who's there?
Warner.
Warner who?
Warner you coming
out to play?

Knock–knock.
Who's there?
Warren.
Warren who?
Warren my birthday suit.

Knock–knock.
Who's there?
Warren.
Warren who?
I'm Warren out!

Knock–knock.
Who's there?
Warren D.
Warren D. who?
Warren D. world are you?

Knock–knock.
Who's there?
Warrior.
Warrior who?
Warrior been all my life?

235

Knock–knock.
  Who's there?
Warsaw.
  Warsaw who?
Warsaw Knock-Knock
joke I ever heard.

Knock–knock.
  Who's there?
Wash out.
  Wash Out who?
Wash Out, I'm coming in!

Knock–knock.
  Who's there?
Wash.
  Wash who?
Wash you there,
Charlie?

Knock–knock.
  Who's there?
Water.
  Water who?
Water be ashamed of yourself
for living in a dump like this!

236

Knock–knock.
  Who's there?
Water.
  Water who?
Water friends for?

Knock–knock.
  Who's there?
Watts.
  Watts who?
Watts up, Doc?

Knock–knock.
  Who's there?
Wayne.
  Wayne who?
I'm Wayne D. Outfield.

Knock–knock.
  Who's there?
Weasel.
  Weasel who?
"Weasel while you work . . ."

Knock–knock.
Who's there?
Wednesday.
Wednesday who?
"Wednesday saints go
marching in . . ."

Knock–knock.
Who's there?
Weirdo.
Weirdo who?
Weirdo you think
you're going?

Knock–knock.
Who's there?
Welcome.
Welcome who?
Welcome up and see
me sometime.

Knock–knock.
Who's there?
Wendy.
Wendy who?
"Wendy wind blows,
the cradle will rock . . ."

Knock–knock.
Who's there?
Wendy Katz.
Wendy Katz who?
Wendy Katz away, the mice will play.

Knock–knock.
Who's there?
Wheelbarrow.
Wheelbarrow who?
Wheelbarrow some money and go on a trip.

Knock–knock.
Who's there?
Whitmore.
Whitmore who?
Whitmore can I say after I say I'm sorry?

Knock–knock.
Who's there?
Whitney.
Whitney who?
Whitney have to say to me?

Knock–knock.
Who's there?
Werner.
Werner who?
Werner you going to grow up?

Knock–knock.
Who's there?
Whelan.
Whelan who?
That's all Whelan good, but I still think you're a nut.

Knock–knock.
Who's there?
Whittier.
Whittier who?
Whittier think my chances are for getting inside?

Knock–knock.
Who's there?
Who.
Who who?
Terrible echo in here,
isn't there?

Knock–knock.
Who's there?
Widow.
Widow who?
A widow kid.

Knock–knock.
Who's there?
Willard.
Willard who?
Willard be too late if I
come back in an hour?

Knock–knock.
Who's there?
Wiener.
Wiener who?
Wiener takes all.

Knock–knock.
Who's there?
William Tell.
William Tell who?
William Tell your mommy
to come to the door?

Knock–knock.
Who's there?
Will F.
Will F. who?
Will F. Iron.

Knock–knock.
Who's there?
Willoughby.
Willoughby who?
Willoughby my
Valentine?

Knock–knock.
Who's there?
Willie.
Willie who?
Willie or won't he?

Knock–knock.
Who's there?
Wilson.
Wilson who?
Wilson body let me in?

Knock–knock.
Who's there?
Winnie.
Winnie who?
Winnie you going to
open the door?

Knock–knock.
Who's there?
Winott.
Winott who?
Winott leave your
brain to science?
Maybe they can
find a cure for it.

Knock-knock.
　Who's there?
Wire.
　Wire who?
Wire we telling Knock-Knock jokes?

Knock–knock.
　Who's there?
Wooden.
　Wooden who?
Wooden you like to know!

Knock–knock.
　Who's there?
Wienie.
　Wienie who?
Wienie more jokes like these!

Knock–knock.
　Who's there?
Archibald.
　Archibald who?
Archibald real tears when he
read these Knock-Knock jokes.

Knock–knock.
 Who's there?
Wolf.
 Wolf who?
Wolf-er goodness sake,
Grandma, what
big teeth you
have!

Knock–knock.
 Who's there?
Woody.
 Woody who?
Woody lady of the house
please open the door?

Knock–knock.
 Who's there?
Woody.
 Woody who?
Woody you care
who this is?

Knock–knock.
Who's there?
Wyatt.
Wyatt who?
Wyatt the world do I
bother to talk to you?

Knock–knock.
Who's there?
Wyden.
Wyden who?
Wyden you tell me
you were a werewolf?

Knock–knock.
Who's there?
Wynn.
Wynn who?
Wynn a few–lose a few.

Knock-Knock!

Knock–knock.
　Who's there?
X.
　X who?
X (Eggs) Benedict!

Knock–knock.
　Who's there?
X.
　X who?
X (Eggs) for breakfast.

Knock–knock.
　Who's there?
Xavier.
　Xavier who?
Xavier breath!
I'm not leaving.

Knock–knock.
　Who's there?
Xavier.
　Xavier who?
Xavier self!

Knock–knock.
Who's there?
Xenia.
Xenia who?
Xenia open the door
last week!

Knock–knock.
Who's there?
Oh Mama!
Oh Mama who?
Oh Mama-stake
(oh, my mistake)!

Knock–knock.
Who's there?
Xenia.
Xenia who?
Xenia stealing my
Mad Magazine.

Knock-Knock!

Knock–knock.
Who's there?
Yates.
Yates who?
Crazy Yates (Eights)!

Knock–knock.
Who's there?
Yeti.
Yeti who?
Yeti-nother Knock-Knock joke!

Knock–knock.
Who's there?
Yogurt.
Yogurt who?
Yogurt to be joking!

Knock–knock.
Who's there?
Arno.
Arno who?
Arno you don't!

Knock–knock.
　Who's there?
Yoko.
　Yoko who?
Yoko jump in the lake.

Knock–knock.
　Who's there?
Yokohama.
　Yokohama who?
Yokohama (you can have my) place in line!

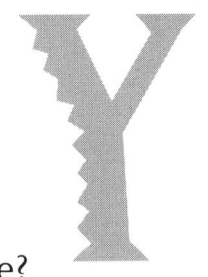

Knock–knock.
　Who's there?
Yucatan.
　Yucatan who?
Yucatan dollars to pay the taxi?

Knock–knock.
　Who's there?
Yokum.
　Yokum who?
"Yokum a long way, baby . . ."

Knock–knock.
　Who's there?
Yucca.
　Yucca who?
Yucca be arrested for impersonating a human being.

Knock–knock.
　Who's there?
Yukon.
　Yukon who?
Yukon (you can't) teach an old dog new tricks!

Knock–knock.
   Who's there?
Yolette.
   Yolette who?
Would Yolette me in the door, please?

   Knock–knock.
     Who's there?
Wilma.
     Wilma who?
Wilma jokes make you open the door?

      Knock–knock.
       Who's there?
Ozzie.
       Ozzie who?
Ozzie (I see) I'm going to be out
here all night.

        Knock–knock.
         Who's there?
Yukon.
         Yukon who?
Yukon say that again!

Y

Knock–knock.
> Who's there?

Yul.
> Yul who?

Yul look wonderful.
Who is your embalmer?

Knock–knock.
> Who's there?

Yule.
> Yule who?

Yule never guess.

Knock–knock.
> Who's there?

Yuma.
> Yuma who?

The Good Yuma man.

Knock–knock.
> Who's there?

Yuri.
> Yuri who?

Yuri mind me of
the Liberty Bell—
half-cracked.

Knock-Knock!

Knock–knock.
   Who's there?
Zany.
   Zany who?
Zany body out there?!

Knock–knock.
   Who's there?
Zelda.
   Zelda who?
Zelda family jewels!

Knock–knock.
   Who's there?
Zenka.
   Zenka who?
Zenka you for your
kind words.

Knock–knock.
    Who's there?
Zinc.
      Zinc who?
Zinc or swim!

Knock–knock.
    Who's there?
Zinc.
      Zinc who?
Zinc of you all
the time!

Knock–knock.
    Who's there?
Zipper and Zipper.
      Zipper and Zipper who?
"Zipper D. Doodah and Zipper D.A. . . ."

Knock–knock.
    Who's there?
Zinnia.
      Zinnia who?
There's method
Zinnia madness.

Z

Knock–knock.
    Who's there?
Zits.
    Zits who?
Zits down and
concentrate.

Knock–knock.
    Who's there?
Zoe.
    Zoe who?
Zoe (so we)
meet again!

Knock–knock.
    Who's there?
Zoo.
    Zoo who?
Zoo long for now!

Knock–knock.
    Who's there?
Cy.
    Cy who?
Cy O'Nara
(Sayonara)!

Knock–knock.
    Who's there?
Zuccarelli.
    Zuccarelli who?
Zuccarelli long time
to get to the last
Knock-Knock
joke!

253

INDEX